Marketing The Romance

GW00391033

by Liam Livings

What other authors say about Marketing the Romance by Liam Livings

'I loved the informal chatty style. It was like getting together with a friend over coffee for a good pep talk. Clear action plans to follow broken down into manageable chunks. It made a daunting task seem less daunting, and even (dare I say it) fun.' (Elisabeth Hobbes, Harlequin Mills and Boon Historical author)

'Who knew a book on marketing could be so entertaining? Liam Livings has somehow managed to make learning about a subject I would normally avoid like the plague accessible, informative and thoroughly enjoyable. If you're a romance author (or any author really) and you want to know how to market your books effectively and strategically (while also avoiding getting sucked into the black hole that is social media) you need to buy this book! I guarantee you will not regret it. And you might actually sell more books too!' (Heidi Rice, USA Today bestselling author, published by Harlequin Mills and Boon Modern and Harlequin Mira UK)

'Liam Livings has penned an invaluable resource for both published and unpublished romance authors. It is highly readable and packed with practical, relevant advice to help even the least marketing-savvy author understand the importance of taking ownership of their own marketing strategy and developing a smarter approach to marketing. Liam's clear, structured approach helps to demystify an often confusing subject and, with the use of genuine examples, he provides real insight into the whys and wherefores of marketing.' (Janice Preston, Harlequin Mills and Boon Historical author)

'A fantastic book for any romance writer trying to find their readers. Practical, detailed, and fun to read. Liam is incredibly knowledgeable about marketing and romantic fiction, and communicates that knowledge with passion and humour.' (Alison May, RONA nominated romantic fiction author and creative writing tutor)

'I wish I had a how-to-guide for marketing romance writing when I first began as an author! Inspiration and good writing are only half the battle – marketing and social media are an integral part of becoming a successful author. Thank goodness someone put it together for the rest of us – Liam Livings' Marketing The Romance is a great guide for learning how to market your romance novels.' (Lara Temple, Harlequin Mills and Boon Historical author)

'There's more to marketing than promoting your finished book, and this highly readable and romance genre-specific guide sets out clearly what you need to be doing to maximise sales. Includes the best explanation I've seen yet of what "author branding" actually means.' (JL Merrow, award-winning gay romance author)

'Practical, useful and sensible advice about marketing your romance novel – whether you're with a traditional publisher or you're an independent – written in a clear, friendly and down-to-earth manner. I learned a lot from it, and have much better ideas about how to restructure my website as a result!' (Kate Hardy, multi-award nominated Harlequin Mills and Boon Medical and Cherish author)

'An absolutely essential marketing guide for today's romance author. Highly recommended! Straight-forward, clear and packed full of tips, advice and research-based strategy to help you get your books noticed!' (Mandy Baggot bestselling and award-winning romance author)

'Practical and jargon-free, Liam's witty take on marketing is gloriously do-able.' (Virginia Heath, RONA nominated Harlequin Mills and Boon Historical author)

'I definitely feel a lot clearer about it [marketing]. I think it's one of those things that no one really talks about, at least not many other writers do and not in this depth. Having read this I feel like there is some structure or plan that I could tailor to my work. I think I like that this is a set of guidelines rather than a prescriptive list of must-do's so I can tailor it to my needs. I loved this! As well as giving some solid advice, it was fun to read with clear examples of what to do. I can't wait for my next book launch so I can try some of this stuff out.' (Alex Jane, male male romance author)

'I thoroughly enjoyed the book. It takes complex marketing theory and makes it accessible and understandable by relating it directly to writing romance. I particularly like that each chapter ends with not only a summary of the key points, but things to consider and do as this really encourages reflection and application. It does de-mystify marketing because it puts it into a context that I can understand – romance. Too often I have read marketing books and just zoned out because it seems so complicated and often I can't see the point. What this does is uses not only romance to explain the techniques, but every day situations. I think that the information is well structured and cumulative. It layers the complexity in bit by bit so that by the time you are reading the really complicated stuff you are okay with it. This is the book that I have been waiting for. Wonderful, conversational style of writing that draws you in and hits you with complex concepts in a way that is completely accessible and understandable. This, coupled with your significant knowledge of not only marketing, but the romance industry and the psychology of romance reading, delivers a first rate, entertaining book that will be endlessly useful and well used. Bravo!' (Ruby Moone, historical gay romance author)

'What a fabulous book. It's great to see a marketing book, specifically for authors that really takes things back to basics and doesn't assume the reader understands the terminology beforehand. It's also encouraging to see comparisons in other industries to get the hang of how to implement in the book world. I really enjoyed it and found it useful.' (Lorna Stickland, RNA New Writers' Scheme member)

'It was fascinating. It will take a bit of assimilating but yes I have learned a lot...This is a text book but the style is so engaging it feels more like a novel. Good sound basic principles – not the flashy make a fortune with this algorithm (which will probably change tomorrow) type of book. Practical examples explain things so well. A godsend for confused romance authors!' (Josie Bonham, romance author)

'If I needed to make one myself (let's face it, I DO need to!) the book gives me a step by step guide to making a plan (and action points). It also shows that a systematic marketing plan is a lot of work. The fact that it focuses on the romance genre specifically, is good...Overall, it's a good balance between being accessible and actually explaining the thinking that goes into making marketing plans...I've read a lot of 'ways to market your novel' type books and posts and it's rare to see the organised approach [it's] taking. How to approach the data is often the bit that's missing and [it's] covered really well.' (Rhoda Baxter, multi-award nominated romance author)

'I particularly liked the way [Liam] ended the chapters with things to remember, consider and do. I also like your mostly informal style which I think helps to demystify book marketing for the lay person a good read and [Liam's] expertise came across well.' (Julie Stock, independent contemporary romance author)

'I wish I'd had this book at the start of my publishing career.' (Sue Brown, male male romance author)

Published by Fluffy Cat Publishing

Cover by T N Westcott

Dedication

Welcome to my book, but before I get to the real reason you're here, there's a few people who deserve a damned good thanking.

Thanks to the lovely people at the Romantic Novelists' Association (RNA) Southern Chapter who I met in March 2017. I gave a talk about marketing and the romance market and a few of the authors there said it was the first time they'd actually understood marketing and asked why didn't I write a book, expanding on my talk. Reader, I wrote it; this is that book! Charlie Cochrane introduced me to the Southern Chapter and everyone there was very friendly and welcoming. Plus, the Italian buffet was delish too. Until we were ushered out by the waiters who wanted to close – I am that much of a chatterbox!

Thanks to my RNA friends who've helped by beta-reading the book, giving me helpful suggestions when I couldn't see the marketing wood from the promotional trees. I need to thank everyone who read the advance reader copy and has given me wonderful quotes which have been duly added to the covers and inside of the book.

Without the RNA I wouldn't know any of these generous, helpful, knowledgeable people. So for that, the RNA itself gets its own paragraph.

Thanks to Tim, who has helped with the production of the book, designed the cover, and did all the technical things that terrified me.

And finally, last but absolutely not least, thanks to you, the reader who's bought a copy of this book. I hope it's enjoyable, useful, practical, and helps you take charge of marketing your books.

Love and light,
Liam Livings xx

CONTENTS

Table of Contents

CHAPTER 1 - Introduction

So why listen to me talking about marketing for the romance genre?

I have a level 6 professional diploma in marketing from the Chartered Institute of Marketing (CIM) which is the internationally recognised professional body based in the UK for marketing. I've worked in various communications and marketing roles since 2008 and have supported a national conference for GLBTQ fiction with its marketing since 2013. I helped to increase its delegate numbers from approximately 60 to 150, at which point we decided to cap the attendance to maintain the event's intimate feeling. I've also helped a publisher put together a marketing strategy and marketing plan (I'll explain what these mean later in the book, don't panic).

I have been a published romance author since 2013, writing gay fiction (with a romantic element) and gay / male male romance. I have a Master of Arts in creative writing, with commendation, from Kingston University; during which my creative pieces were all romances, and my specialist subject was the romance genre which meant I extensively researched the genre.

Why marketing for romance authors?

According to the RNA, romance is the most popular genre of fiction. (RNA, n.d.) Business of Consumer Book Publishing found romance was the largest share of the consumer market at 13.5 percent. (in Jeffers, 2008)

As a genre too, 'romantic fiction is the punching bag of the literary world.' (Mayo, 2014) Its readers are often 'the laughing stock of literary commentators.'(ibid) Among other insults, romance is described as 'preposterous. Nothing is at stake. So you can just enjoy what you can enjoy, and then forget it.' (Gottlieb in Faircloth, 2017)

'When are you going to write proper books?' people say to the romance author. People criticise romance for being poorly written and for selling a lie to the 84% female readers. (RWA, 2014) This completely misunderstands the whole point of romance: escape and being effortless to read.

'What a lovely use of a semi-colon!' or 'I loved how the author didn't use any present participles in the start of the novel.' Or how about 'I really enjoyed the complete absence of perception filters and dangling modifiers best of all!' Said no reader of popular fiction. Ever! Most readers of most fiction don't give a monkey's about the beautiful prose and wonderful phrasing; they're interested in the characters, their emotions, the story, the romance. I'll come back to this later in more detail to show how you can use this to your advantage when writing your next romance novel.

Romance has a double whammy for criticism: it's popular (most things that are popular tend to come in for some pretty harsh critique from the so-called critics – just look at the difference between critics' ratings and audience ratings for some films on *Rotten Tomatoes*) and it's a genre almost exclusively written and enjoyed by women. Things that women do and enjoy also tend to get criticised more and valued less than those deemed to be 'men's stuff'. I'll just pause here to give an example of how long this has been happening. Indulge me if you will, please? I'll try to illustrate my points throughout this book with real life examples. They may be from the car industry (as it's something I know well) they may be from books themselves, and they may be from something totally different but the point is to illustrate what I'm saying. I want to demystify marketing and will always explain 'technical terms' using examples.

Anyway, so back to my example. In the sixties there was a pay dispute at the Ford factory. The women who sewed the car seats took industrial action because they felt their jobs should be graded and paid the same as the men's because they were both as skilled. The fact that the women were sewing seat covers and the men were riveting doors together was immaterial. Eventually, this led to the equal pay act of 1970 which basically says that equal work of equal value regardless of who does it, should be paid the same amount.

Romance is a maligned and criticised popular genre and is – I believe, due to its popularity – based on the principles of marketing. I was the only pupil in my MA in creative writing year who was writing popular genre fiction. Out of about twenty of us, just me. Everyone else in the prose section was writing literary fiction. As part of my MA, I did quite a bit of research about romance as a genre, what makes it work, its conventions and the structure of a romance novel and through reading Janice Radway's 1984 research study *Reading The Romance,* where she spoke to a group of American women about their romance reading preferences, *I* understood why readers enjoy it so voraciously. Radway's study is the only of its kind about romance readers and is why I've quoted it quite a bit during this book. After all this reading I came to the conclusion that romance is a very commercial genre that's specifically designed to keep customers coming back for more and more. *Giving customers what they want and making money from it.*

The fact that romance is a popular genre means it's sold to many readers. To achieve this, the publishers must be doing something right. The way they've done this is to become a marketing-led industry before there really was a phrase for it. The traditional model of publishing would be to find a wonderful story and then try to find an audience willing to read it.

Romance turned this on its head in the sixties with the introduction of category romances or lines of similar stories. In fancy marketing speak it's called semi-programmed issue. This basically means you develop stories within a framework

12

for an already existing and hungry audience. I'll come back to this later to explain in more detail.

Marketing is a much misunderstood profession. People think it's all about sales and selling stuff to people. But marketing is so much more than that; *it's about giving the customers what they want, profitably.* There's more to it than that, but getting down to brass tacks that's about it. Doesn't that sound similar to what the romance genre does too?

What this book is
This book is intended to be a guide for romance authors, and aspiring romance authors to make sense of marketing, explain all the technical marketing jargon in easy to understand ways and help authors learn how they can apply marketing principles to their own books.

It is intended to help romance authors understand what they can do to be smarter with their efforts to market their books. Marketing is much more than just sales, and the things romance authors can do to better market their books are many and varied. I do not expect all romance authors who read this book to go out and start doing every one of the things discussed. That would be impossible.

The purpose of the book is to explain how broad marketing is, help romance authors know and demystify some strategic systematic approaches they can take to being smarter at marketing, and then decide which one(s) to do themselves. If you finish this book with a few tips for how to approach marketing differently because you finally 'get' why you're doing it, and how to do it systemically, then that will be a win as far as I'm concerned.

Because marketing is so wide, as a discipline, and because, understandably, authors are very fixated on their book sales, it can be very easy to run off and try a little bit of this, and a bit more of that to try and sell more books. This is both scattergun, and often means jumping straight to *tactics* without thinking *strategically* or basing your actions on evidence from *research*. OK, so I just threw in three marketing speak words in that last sentence. Marketing jargon klaxon! *Tactics, strategically, research*.

Right, *tactics* is what you're actually doing on a day to day basis. To sell more books you read that Twitter is the new thing, so you get an account and then 'do' Twitter like there's no tomorrow. You've jumped straight to the doing without thinking about it *strategically* (what are you trying to achieve) first.

Once you've considered things *strategically*, you may decide that what you actually need to do isn't Twitter, it's something else (talking to your local library, joining some Facebook groups for example).

Plus, all decisions in marketing should be made on the basis of *research* which will give you evidence. Research sounds very high and mighty but honestly, in the age of the internet, you can do so much 'desk research' which basically means Googling things, without leaving the comfort of your own laptop and office.

So hopefully that's *tactics, strategically* and *research* covered in terms of marketing jargon!

Using an everyday analogy, imagine you wanted to move house because you need another bedroom. If you were to jump straight to tactics you would put the house on the market, rub your hands with glee at a great offer, and then sell without finding somewhere else to live (because you're so sure you just need to sell your house and worry about the next steps later). So now you're living in a caravan looking for somewhere to buy with another bedroom and lo and behold you find out that to live in the same area (because you like it and the kids are at school there) and get another bedroom, it's way more than you sold your house for, and more than you can borrow on a mortgage. So you've achieved the tactic (of selling your house) without thinking it through strategically on the basis of research.

Taking a more *strategic* approach to the fact that you need another bedroom, here's how you'd approach things:

1) You think *strategically* about your options for acquiring another bedroom: moving house, extending your existing house, partitioning off your largest bedroom, converting your dining room into a downstairs sleeping area.

2) Now let's do some *research* to inform the decision: look at the cost of moving house and buying a house in your area with another bedroom already, the cost of building an extension, and the cost of partitioning or converting existing rooms.

3) Now, based on the *research* you knock out some options due to them being too expensive or time-consuming (there will always be reasons to discount some options these are just an example). This leaves you with the options of building an extension and converting the dining room into a bedroom. Your final decision is to convert the dining room (this is a *tactic*) which gives you an immediate solution to your lack of a bedroom, and in the meantime you will save money to pay for a loft conversion in the medium term because you now know (based on research) that building a loft is quicker and cheaper than the price of moving and buying a bigger house in your area.

Remember! Don't jump straight to *tactics* without thinking *strategically* and doing your *research* first!

What this book isn't

I think it's worth here having a disclaimer about what I can't do in writing this book. This book is not a guide for how to write the next *50 Shades of Grey* or *Gone Girl* or *The Girl on the Train* or *Harry Potter* and sell a million. Each of these has their own reasons for doing so well.

The Girl on the Train was Paula Hawkins' fifth book. The others had sold pretty modestly and for some reason (it may have been having 'girl' in the title if you look at other bestsellers for that year but I'm sure there was more to it than that) it sold so much better than the others.

50 Shades of Grey was a publishing phenomenon and it's also worth pointing out that before it was published traditionally it had been published online as *Twilight* fan fiction.

Fan fiction is where you use existing fictional characters and write your own story. You can't sell fan fiction because the author who created the original characters owns the rights to those characters.

EL James wrote a sexier version of Bella and Edward from *Twilight* and posted chapters on fan fiction sites gradually gathering more and more enthusiastic readers. Then she published it through a small publisher, having distanced her story from *Twilight* – changing character names and characteristics etc. And only then, when it was selling modestly well, was it picked up by a mainstream publisher. Most massive sales successes don't really come out of nowhere, there's usually a story behind them as I've just shown.

Some massively selling books happen to be riding the crest of a wave of the current trend at the time: mindfulness, hygge[1], baking, having 'girl' in the title, cosy tea shops, wizards etc.

And on top of this, there's also the need to have a great big dollop of luck as well.

Ethel Merman ends her fabulous 1978 autobiography in a similar vein, which goes to show that time doesn't change that much; with my italics to emphasise the point:

1

Hygge 'is a Norwegian and Danish word for a mood of coziness and comfortable conviviality with feelings of wellness and contentment. (Wikipedia, n.d.)

'Because of all the success I've enjoyed, I'm often asked to advise young people who want to go into the theater. But truthfully, I don't feel that I have the secret. I'd like to say, Work hard, never give up, keep trying, that's the secret. But that's not true. In my case things have pretty much been handed to me.

I'll pat myself on the back and admit *I have talent.* Beyond that, *I just happened to be in the right place at the right time…*

Once I had the attention, all I had to do was deliver.

I do think you have to make that big dent to begin with.' (Merman, 1978, p264)

Is there a guarantee that the marketing efforts you make will sell more books?

And, more importantly, can I tell you inarguably that if you follow all these points you'll become a bestseller?

There are no guarantees in life except death and taxes. And no, I can't make these two claims, and any marketeer who does is lying.

However, although there's no guarantee that telling people about your book will actually sell more copies, I can tell you for absolute certain that people definitely won't buy your book if they've never heard of it.

So that's the end of the first chapter. I hope that was useful and interesting and hasn't bamboozled you with lots of marketing jargon words. I'm going to end each chapter with these three headings: *Things to remember, Things to consider, Things to do.*

So you might like to pause at the end of each chapter and work through these three sections.

Things to remember
- Tactics – something you do on a day to day basis, tweeting, blogging, deciding to do a talk at a library. It is an action.

- Strategic – taking a step back and thinking what you're trying to achieve overall with what you're doing.
- Research – looking online, asking customers, asking other authors, to find evidence in answer to a research question for example: How much is the most popular e-book price in £?

Things to consider
- Think about approaches to marketing your books you've taken and ask yourself if you've done it by going straight to tactics, or did you first do some research and take a step back to think strategically?
- Think about how you could have approached your marketing efforts differently by being strategic and doing some research.

Things to do
- Make a list of marketing jargon / new terms you've read in this chapter and note down what they mean. Not all of them will have been explained in this chapter because I said a few times I'd come back to certain topics in more detail.
- Think about what two to three things you'd like to know how to do to help you market your books and write these down. Keep these in mind when reading the rest of the book.

CHAPTER 2 - What is marketing?

Marketing isn't something that happens 'over there' and is done by 'other people'. The other people being marketing consultants, publishers, various other experts. The main purpose of this book is to help romance authors see that marketing, in its widest sense, is something that you *should* and *can* do for yourself, every single day.

Sending out ARCs (advance reader copies) of your books to get reviews from review blogs, is promotion and is basically admin. Having a company do that for you, if you're a busy author, is a good use of money, and saves the author's time.

However, there's much more to marketing than getting reviews, or promotion. And they are all much more than admin, and are therefore best done by the person with the most interest in the most important part of marketing – the product. They're your books, so why wouldn't you want to be in charge (or at least have a tight steer) on how they are marketed?

Marketing is something the modern author, with an online presence, should be doing a little of. Every. Single. Day. Yes, even if you're lucky enough to have a big publisher assigning you a PR person and organising for your books to be in supermarkets etc, you can still ensure that everything you do is with marketing in mind. How, you're probably asking?

That's where the tools and frameworks I'll describe in this book come in useful. They are just a way of structuring your thinking, in a systematic, strategic way. And they are all things you, as an author, can work through yourself, either to implement on your own, or to work with a publisher to implement in the future.

Marketing is not simply promotion; it is much more than that. Promotion is just one of the 7 Ps of marketing.

Marketing vs sales

People often think that marketing is only about sales because that's the bit that feels most obvious when you think about marketing. You imagine someone shouting on a market stall selling you some apples and when you buy them that's what marketing is.

Sales, according to dictionary.com is, 'The business or activity of selling goods or services.' (dictionary.com, n.d.)

Marketing, according to the Chartered Institute of Marketing is, 'the management process responsible for identifying, anticipating and satisfying customer requirements profitably.' (The Chartered Institute of Marketing, 2015)

And before you get all 'I'm an artist and I write what I want and don't need to know what customers want because that would compromise my creativity' can I just say that by its nature, romance is a popular genre with its own genre expectations. If you want to stand a better chance of selling more books, knowing the genre expectations and taking on customer feedback can help you decide consciously whether or not to listen to it. At least when you know the romance genre's expectations you can then knowingly decide to break them, rather than doing it accidentally and wondering why you've got an avalanche of one star reviews.

The basic requirements as an author

If you're an author and you want to market your products (books) to your customers, you need at least a website and or blog and you also need some social media presence.

Website

This is basically your online home, where customers should come to in order to find out what you're doing, your next book, where they can buy them, to read reviews of your books.

Imagine it's like your readers coming round your house for a cup of tea. There are plenty of website builders for free or not very much money that allow you to tailor it to how you want it to look. Your website should reflect who you are as an author, what you write, what your brand is. This means visually with colours, pictures as well as the actual words on your website.

What is Branding?

Marketing jargon klaxon!

Brand is something that's bandied about all the time assuming that everyone understands what it means. But really, what is a brand?

A brand isn't a logo, or a strapline, or an icon, or a jingle. Although a brand includes all or some of these elements.

A brand is a promise to a customer about their product or service. (Marsh, 2013)

It's important that the product lives up to the brand or that promise is broken and the customer probably won't come back for more.

Imagine you want to buy some new clothes for a summer holiday. You go into a high street shop, say Primark, whose *strapline* is 'look good, pay less' and is plastered on their lorries, bags etc, to buy a pair of jeans. *A strapline is a series of words that sum up the brand simply and clearly.* You find a pair you like, try them on and they definitely make you look good (that's half of the brand promise fulfilled) but when you get to the cashier you're shocked to find the jeans cost £150. So that's the 'pay less' bit of the brand promise broken. You would be unlikely to return again.

Let's take Gucci as a complete contrast. Their slogan is 'Quality is Remembered Long After the Price is Forgotten.' (Wijitha, 2009) With Gucci you're expecting the product to be expensive, the brand's slogan promises this to you. It says that the most important thing is the quality because you'll soon forget the price (which I'll suggest is only relevant to those customers for whom money really is no object). You buy a lovely jumper in Gucci and it costs £500 but you don't care because soon enough you'll forget the price and simply get on with enjoying the wonderful quality of your purchase. So far the 'price is forgotten' promise is being upheld. And then, horror of horrors, you wash your new jumper after wearing it once and spilling some tea down the front. Taking it out of the washing machine you're horrified to find that it has gone all bobbly and misshapen and the colours have faded. Crash! Bang! Wallop! That's the sound of the 'quality is remembered' promise coming crashing down around your ears. Again, you'd probably not return for another product.

Let's return to Primark now and imagine you buy a lovely jumper and it costs £10. You wear it for that season, it makes you feel fabulous, it's on trend, you look good and then at the end of the season after it's been washed a dozen times it's faded, a bit bobbly and misshapen. Well, Primark has upheld their brand promise, you've looked good and paid less. You use the jumper as a duster / to polish your car / take it to a charity shop hence moving on from it so you can buy a new one from Primark's next season.

Imagine, if you will, that we go back to Gucci to buy a pair of jeans (a snip at only £750) and they become your go-to jeans when you're not sure what else to wear.

They make you feel fabulous. They're timeless classics. You go for meals-out, nights-in, dates, job interviews, everything and these jeans come along with you like faithful friends.

Finally, ten years later, they're looking a bit faded and passé so you take them to a charity shop but you're happy in the knowledge that despite the exorbitant price, their quality saw you through many happy years and by this point you have indeed forgotten how much they cost. Gucci brand promise delivered!

Coming back to authors again, if you write 1940s sagas set in the East End of London then your website should reflect that. Your blogs should be about issues related to the 1940s in the East End of London. The colours, pictures, logo, everything about you online should be relevant for, yes you guessed it, 1940s in the East End of London.

If, however, you write glitzy bonkbusters in the style of Jackie Collins, your website should be a bit racier. You may blog and write about sex a bit, since you probably include it in your books. Have some glitzy pictures of big racing cars, a Rolls Royce in a swimming pool. You get the idea.

Whatever your author brand, your website should have static content – that stays the same or is changed infrequently: your contact details, your biography, a list of your books you update as and when.

As well as this you should also think about some regularly updating web content – otherwise known as a blog. This gives customers a reason to return to your website regularly. If you went to a shop and it always had the same things displayed in the window you'd soon stop checking it. Your online shop / home must have new things in its window to keep customers coming back for more. While they're looking at your latest blog they may stop by and re-read your list of books and oh look, there's one she doesn't have, or a review she'd not read before.

Blogging is *content marketing*. Marketing jargon klaxon!

Content marketing is where you give something for free with the hope that customers will then buy something. At its most basic level it's free samples in a food shop. You know those free recipe books from manufacturers of flour that seem to use *an awful lot of flour* in them? Content marketing.

The *Michelin Restaurant Guide* is a very early example of content marketing. It was given away for free for lorry drivers to know where to eat at the end of a long day on the road. The idea was that by having Michelin in their minds every day when they ate, when the time came to replace the tyres on the lorry they'd immediately think of Michelin as a trusted brand.

As an author your product is your words, so writing useful interesting articles on your blog is a way of readers getting to sample your writing. If they like what they read, the style, the voice, they're more likely to take a chance and buy a book than if they'd not read anything of yours before. A word of caution about blogging: all of your blogging should be in line with your brand as an author and link back to the sort of books you write. If the link is quite tenuous that's OK, as long as the blogging doesn't undermine your author brand. I'll explain with some author examples I've totally made up…

Imagine you're an author who writes sweet male / female romances set in a rural idyll. If you started blogging about why you loved reading *Hot Head*, a male / male romance about two male firefighters having lots of very explicit sex, then you may alienate some of your readers. I'm not saying don't enjoy reading *Hot Head*, or lesbian tentacle porn, or male pregnancy fiction or whatever you want to read, just don't blog about it with the same name as you're writing sweet rural romances.

Similarly, if you write racy stories about male cops / firemen / cowboys getting it on with other hot male cops / firemen / cowboys then maybe don't write a series of blogs about why you joined the local Women's Institute branch and how your jam was the envy of the village. (I'm exaggerating for effect!)

If your stories include, as well as sexy firemen and cops, a lot about families and relationships, then feel free to blog about your family, relationships, etc. But always ask yourself 'is this going to reinforce or damage my author brand' before writing it. Readers will love to read about your views on things, your experiences, your writing, anything really, as long as it's congruent with your brand. Your products (books) too should always fulfil your brand promise, otherwise it's like opening a packet of cornflakes and finding two pieces of salmon wrapped inside.

Brand for authors isn't always as simple as it only being your author name. For big name authors their brand is most definitely their name: Marian Keyes, Joanna Trollope, Tasmina Perry, Jo Jo Moyes, Adele Parks among many more. How often have you heard someone saying, 'I can't wait to get the next AUTHOR NAME'? Authors are known for writing a certain type of story and so readers come back again and again wanting to relive that same pleasure of reading their books. There's a lot of research around why romance readers return time and time again for basically the same story and I'll come onto that later. I'm not denigrating romance, but really, the basic story is: boy meets girl (or boy meets boy, or girl meets girl), boy and girl (or boy and boy...you get the point) have a series of obstacles to prevent them being together, boy and girl overcome obstacles, boy and girl are together. The important differences come in the setting, the characters, their conflicts etc. But the basic story of a romance is the same time and time again.

Not all authors' names are their brand because they're not a big enough name. Instead they rely on their visuals to cluster themselves with similar authors. Go to Amazon and find an author whose books you love. Look underneath to the 'other customers also bought' section. I bet you'll find some very similar covers using very similar typefaces and colours. The publishers of those authors have deliberately used similar visuals to appeal to readers of similar books.

A while ago there was a series of literary fiction books with covers showing a woman standing in front of a large house partly obscured by fog and a bird cage rested on the floor next to the woman. Just look at the *50 Shades of Grey* imitators, they're all pretty similar. In the male male romance genre there's an awful lot of covers with bare male chests on display. Look at the post war memories books, lots of sepia pictures of cobbled streets. How about the proliferation of cupcake / cosy / cottage typed books that are popular at the moment – they all have very similar covers. This is deliberate.

If you're not a big enough name for your name alone to be a stand out brand, and if you have any control over your covers then I would suggest you ask your publisher to imitate similar authors in your genre. Imitation is the greatest form of flattery, isn't it!

And finally, there's another type of brand, distinct from author name or author visuals; there's the publisher brand. Here I'm talking about large publishers with an established brand for publishing certain types of books over a sustained period of time. These publishers have segmented their products (segmented means divided up into different groups of customers, more on this later) to sell a series of lines, or categories of romance. So the reader is less interested in the author per se, but more interested in reading a specific category of romance – supernatural, sweet, set in a hospital, international locations etc. The picture and colouring of the book cover are consistent across each category, reassuring the reader they'll get cornflakes when they open the packet and not smoked salmon.

Before you get all uppity about a book being a form of art and it not being the same as a packet of cornflakes – that may be the case with literary fiction (although fewer people read that) but in category romances, the author names tend to be much smaller because in this type of branding, the author name is second or third to the publisher / line's brand.

Authors who write these category romances tend to say so in their bios and on their websites. This again reinforces the fact that the category is the main branding they are linked to rather than their own author name. Pick up a Mills & Boon Medical or True Love book and notice the size of the author's name against the size of the title, the colouring that shows it's Medical or True Love. In order of size on the cover it will go: picture > category branding > book title > author name.

I've explained these different types of branding, not to say one is better than the other; simply they are about where you are with your writing career, what sort of books you write, and who your publisher is. Knowing which of these three types of branding you fall under will help you make decisions when branding your website and discussing covers with your publisher, or a cover designer.

Social media

In addition to a website which is your online home, you also need a presence on social media. Think of this as *you, only online*. It should direct readers back to your website, which is your online home.

Now we know all about branding, have a guess what your social media presence should do...Yep, that's right, be *congruent* with your branding.

Make sure your posts across all the social media platforms you use are congruent with your author brand and what you write about. I have a published author friend who's a vicar's wife and she very deliberately stays away from religion and politics on social media as an author. There's a reason we were told as children to avoid politics and religion as dinner party topics.

For some reason, with social media, some people think they have the right to post what they want on their profiles. You absolutely do have the right to post whatever you want as your social media profile. But the difference with making a comment to someone at a dinner party and writing a long ranty post on Facebook or posting a blog, or getting into an argument on Twitter is that the former is gone, once you finish the conversation. The latter is there. Forever. Screen grabs and online sharing means your rant can be around the world in minutes. Publishers look at authors' social media profiles and if they see you're a bit ranty and somewhat off-brand (yes, that important word again) then they're less likely to offer you a publishing contract if there's another author with an equally brilliant manuscript who's much better behaved online.

I stick to the six Cs when I post on social media: cars, cats, cakes, creating words, commenting on books I'm reading, commenting on my life in all its campness. Anything that falls outside of those categories I sit on my hands and fire off an email or text to a trusted friend, but I try not to post about it online.

I know plenty of successful authors who do post about politics and religion and they seem to do all right. My question is, do you want to spend your time and energy having fights with people online when you could be writing instead?

Which social media platforms should I use?

I'm often asked which social media authors should be using. There's Facebook, Twitter, Instagram, Tumblr, Snapchat, Pinterest etc. It's better to pick a few platforms you're comfortable with and use them properly, rather than trying to spread yourself too thinly across all of them. It's worse to have a social media account set up and to never use it than not to have one at all.

I know you can set social media to post across more than one platform at once. So you post on Facebook and it automatically posts to Instagram, Tumblr and Twitter. That's great, but you need to make sure you're checking back in all the different profiles for mentions, replies, questions to your posts. And you also need to make sure your posts actually do work across multiple platforms. Each different social media profile is better at different things than others. Twitter encourages links to external websites. Facebook prefers you keep things 'in' Facebook. Instagram is really focussed on pictures and lots of # people search by. Tumblr tends to have quite a lot of //cough, cough// explicit content; which is not permitted on Facebook, but is on Twitter.

Also, and very importantly, you should try to use the social media platforms (Facebook / Twitter / Instagram etc) *which your readers use*. Short of knocking on people's doors or meeting them in book shops, social media is the main way authors can interact with their readers now. Find out where online your readers (or readers of books similar to yours) hang out, and go there. I have a whole section later on finding your readers which uses a step by step process to identify them, so don't panic, we'll come back to this in more detail.

How do I sell books online?

If you're only using social media to sell your books you're doing something wrong. It's called *social* media, not *selling* media. Use social media to be sociable, to interact with your readers, with other authors and share your brand, what you're about and among all of that interacting and engaging with readers you can also mention if you have a new book out, or share a great review you've had from another reader.

Rather than trying to sell, sell, sell, online you should be trying to engage, engage, engage by being sociable, sociable, sociable.

Imagine you were sitting at a dinner party with friends discussing TV, or the food, or the bypass in the village, whatever. So you're all having a great time and in the middle of it someone takes out a hammer from their bag and says, 'I'm a plumber, do you need me to help put a new bathroom in?'

Kind of kills the conversation, doesn't it?

However, if you were at the dinner party discussing for example, home improvement and someone mentioned how difficult it was to find someone reliable to refit their bathroom, then, and only then, could the plumber mention what he did for a living. It's all about context and how receptive the audience is to you starting to sell.

If you're having a discussion online about favourite books and readers are chipping in and adding more to the list to share with others, it could be a good time, if your book is similar to those discussed, to mention they might like to try your book. However, if they're talking about *EastEnders* and how one of the characters has just come back from the dead and you muscle in and say, 'I've got a great book about jet setting around New York and please can you buy it!' you'll probably be blocked and unfriended and all sorts.

Just imagine if you'd do it in real life, and if the answer is no, then don't do it online. And remember, online is the internet and the internet is forever. Forever.

However, if you make your promotional posts on social media not about your amazing book, or why you're such an amazing author writing all the beautiful words, but about the reader and how your book fits with all these other great things she enjoys in her life – *Strictly Come Dancing*, pictures of hot men, escaping to a beach for a holiday, baking cakes – then you're much more likely to get readers to click on the buy link.

Things to remember
• Branding – is a promise to a customer about a product or service. Make sure your books keep the promise your author brand promises her.
• Strapline – some words to sum up a product's branding simply. This goes with the logo and the colours to form the whole branding together.
• Content marketing – giving away free content with the anticipation that customers will buy content. Blogging is content marketing if it's done congruently with your author brand.

Things to consider
• Have you ever considered what your brand is as an author?
• When you promote your books do you link them to current TV / film / real life events?

• If blogging feels like a lot of work for not much in return, pick a topic you could write a series of short 400 word blogs about, that links back to your author brand, and write them.

Things to do

• Sum up your branding with a series of words. What is your promise that your books give to your readers?

• Write your very own strapline. You don't need to use it, and reading through the rest of the book you'll be able to refine it, but have a go now, write a few straplines you think fit as part of your branding.

CHAPTER 3 - The marketing mix – what it is and why should I care as a romance author?

If, at the moment, you're doing marketing on the hoof – making it up as you go along, not being strategic, and not necessarily basing things on research, and only using your gut instinct – rest assured you're not alone. Most small businesses work this way. And an author, particularly one who's self-publishing her own books, is a small business.

A small business will have an instinctive understanding of what has sold well, what didn't sell so well, you may also feel you know your customers – what she likes, what she doesn't like etc. Just using your gut instinct, you can probably work out that finding out what your customers want and then giving it to them will help you sell more books. In addition it's pretty logical that you'd want to develop new products (books) that do just that. This is all basic common sense. However, coming back to my house moving analogy, it's not very strategic or research based.

The marketing mix is a framework that gives you structure to think through all the elements of marketing I've described above, in a systematic, strategic way. Really you should take this approach for each new product (book). That probably sounds like a lot of work (it isn't because it's probably a couple of hours of working through the marketing mix and writing down your answers to formulate a plan). (The Chartered Institute of Marketing, 2015)

Originally the marketing mix consisted of 4 Ps and then they added another 3 Ps for the service sector, but they're actually applicable in most industries. I'll go through each of them in turn and use examples from the book industry to illustrate my points.

Don't panic! If you don't like the marketing jargon sound of 'marketing mix' just think of it as a list of things to think about when you're going to develop a new product (write a new book). This marketing mix is what I meant by a framework to structure your thinking – a list to follow when you're making decisions and considering options about this.

Product

This can be a physical thing like a car, a T-shirt, a book, or it can also be a service – a flight, a holiday, an insurance policy. We'll come on to how customers want reassurance when the product can't be felt or touched, later under Physical Evidence.

To be marketing-led (and romance as a genre is very marketing-led or it wouldn't be so popular) you need to consider what your customers want from a product, now and in the future and then find out a way to give that to the customers. This may sound like putting the cart before the horse, but how many times has an editor or publisher or agent asked you what your book is similar to? Or what category your book fits under? If they can put it into an existing category they can market it to an existing audience. Think of the category romances sold in their millions by Mills and Boon. How do you find out what your customers want? Well, that's where you do research.

Remember I said all marketing decisions should be backed up by evidence based on research? This is where it starts. Later I have a whole section on research, how you can do it yourself, what you should look for, how you can use that to inform your future products. A perfect product is what's perfect *as far as the customer is concerned,* not the producer. Customers are king / queen.

Let's go back to the clothes shops I described earlier. Do you think the person who bought the cheap jumper in Primark is the same customer who bought the expensive jeans in Gucci? They may have been, but it's very unlikely. The Primark customer's perception of 'value' and 'good' are completely different to the Gucci customer's perceptions of 'value' and 'good'. However, as long as the product the Gucci customer buys meets her perception of 'good' and 'value' she will be happy. It's the same for the Primark customer. There's no point trying to sell your glitzy jet-setting bonkbuster to a customer who only reads 1940s sagas about midwives. Once you understand who your customer is, where she hangs out, what her values are, what she enjoys, what she thinks is 'good' and 'value' then you can start to make sure your books meet those expectations.

And how do we find out all those things about your readers?

Research! Research! Research!

Before continuing with the rest of the marketing mix I'll take a pause to respond to something related to the Product, as the first and most important part of the marketing mix.

What to market before you've written anything

I'm often asked what an author should market before they've written anything. So, it's no coincidence that the marketing mix starts with Product. Without a product you don't have anything to market. Imagine someone standing at a market stall shouting, 'Buy my apples, only 50p a pound!' and when a customer walks up to buy some he sees an empty market stall.

'Sorry, I don't have any apples. I've sold out.'

The customer walks away disappointed, confused and unlikely to return to that market trader again.

However, if the market stall holder had said, 'I'm going to have some apples for sale here next week. They'll be organic, British and include some varieties most other stalls don't stock. Would you like me to call you when I'm back? Here is a flyer with some details. Or would you like me to take your email address and I can drop you a line when I'm all set up?'

Some customers may be more interested. Although he doesn't have anything for sale NOW, he's explaining what his apples will be like, how they're different from everyone else's apples, and starting to build a relationship with customers for the future.

To get fancy with some marketing jargon that is: using his *marketing communications* to *differentiate* himself from other products and using *relationship marketing* principals.

Right, so that's at least three marketing jargon klaxons right there. Taking one at a time.

Marketing communications is anything that communicates with your customers – his flyer in this example. I'll come onto more about these later but this is all you need to know for now.

Differentiating is explaining how your products are different from other customers (and by implication better).

Relationship marketing is about starting to develop an ongoing relationship with your customers rather than just a one-off transaction. You know those reward cards from shops, that's relationship marketing. Not all customers will come back to you, but if you don't ask them, none of them will. If your product interests them and you're personable, you will get some customers coming back to you. And if you take their email addresses you can contact them yourself, so you're not relying on them coming back to you – which is even better.

So, in response to the question, 'What should I market before I've written anything?'

My answer is that the product itself, *the book*, is the most important thing. An author without a book isn't an author. An author without a book is like the millions of people you'll meet who tell you they'd love to write a book if only they had the time. The difference between an author and everyone else is that you've actually written a book.

Or, to put it another way – the ditch ain't dug until you've dug the ditch. The book isn't written until you've written the book.

So, don't forget to write the damned book! But in the meantime, yes you can market yourself as an author – what is your brand about? Start telling people about your book, what it's similar to, if readers like x or y author they may also like your book. If you use the social media and online tips I've already gone through, when you discuss your book with a publisher / agent, you can confidently say you have lots of readers interested in buying the book, that you're confident in engaging with your readers online in a respectful way that's in-line with your brand. These are all music to a publisher's ears.

But, please, dear God, please, don't spend all your time mincing about on social media and blogging about writing the book and not actually writing the damned book!

At the end of the day, if the man turns up every week to the market shouting about his apples, but never brings any, no matter how great his flyer is or how many times he emails people, he will soon have customers ignoring him.

People come to authors to buy their books. Without a book, you are not an author, you're someone who's talking about writing but not actually doing it.

Write. The. Book.

The ditch ain't dug until you've dug the ditch.

That.

Is.

All.

In terms of time spent, before you've finished your first book, I would spend 90% of your writing time actually writing and 10% marketing (in its broadest sense of the word marketing as described throughout this book).

When you have books written, I'd change that to 75% writing and 25% marketing (again, in its broadest sense).

Turning back to the rest of the marketing mix now.

Price

This is the only part of the marketing mix that makes any money. Everything else is a cost in terms of time, or actual hard cash.

If you're traditionally published you will probably have little or no say over the price of your books, so feel free to skip this part if you wish. However, I think it's still worth exploring the issue of price here for everyone regardless of whether you set your own book prices or not.

I went on a three day course with the CIM, called 'Pricing for Product Managers' in 2012 and I'll summarise the main points here:

The price needs to be competitive (from the perspective of the customer, because, as with the product itself, it's all about the customer's point of view). Being competitive doesn't necessarily mean being the cheapest. I saw some research about e-book pricing. $0.99 works out pretty well, as does $2.99 and $3.99 but $1.99 does abysmally. The price of something is as much as a customer is willing to pay for it. Look at house prices or the price of second hand cars to clearly illustrate this.

The price a customer is willing to pay is based on their perceived value of the product.

How much they value the product will be influenced by a number of factors: if it is a new author to them (new authors are unlikely to persuade customers to part with much money, whereas old favourites are probably on customers auto-buy list pretty much regardless of price), how much they usually pay for books (if they only buy e-books or only buy books at reduced price, they're unlikely to pay full price unless it's an auto buy author), their disposable income (books are like other entertainment – cinema, eating out, paid TV subscriptions – discretionary spending. How much a person wants to spend regularly on books will depend on how much they spend in other areas of discretionary entertainment spending).

If something is cheap enough for customers to give it a try, they generally will. If something is a bit more expensive there's a feeling that it is probably of better quality. The problem comes when you fall between the two of these categories. This is why $1.99 is a bit of a dead zone in terms of e-book pricing in the US. It's not cheap enough to think, I'll just give it a go, and it's not expensive enough, near the mainstream published books that are believed to be of superior quality than the indie published books, so people don't try it.

There are three main ways you can price products:
- competitor based
- cost based
- value based

Competitor based pricing is where you look at what your competitors (and by this I mean books similar to yours in the same genre and sub-category) and you decide to price the same, or slightly less, hoping you don't get caught by the issues I've described above. Warning to this approach – this takes out any added value you can give to your customers, particularly if you're indie publishing. It also ignores factors like how big an author name / brand your competitor authors are, even if they're in the same genre as you. In addition, it ignores factors like how long the book itself is, which is also important for readers' perception of value. So, for example a less-known author's book that's 80,000 words could be priced at about the same as a Joanna Trollope or a Marian Keyes well-known author in the same genre, whose book was perhaps only 60,000 words.

Cost based pricing is where you work out how much your product has cost to produce, add a margin in for profit, and then price it accordingly. With e-books this is much harder than say making cakes. I'll use cakes because I've bored myself by using car examples.

If you wanted to sell cakes at a baking sale you would work out your costs of raw ingredients, add in a bit for electricity to cook them and fuel to transport the cakes to the sale, then add in any costs of hiring the bake sale table. Say a cake's raw ingredients cost £2 plus about £1 for the other costs as I've described, that's a total cost of £3. You could aim to sell the cake for £6 and would make a profit of £3 for that cake. I remember Mary Berry reckoned on that sort of multiple when calculating prices to sell cakes at, so she can't be far wrong. If you're self-publishing a paperback, you can work out the cost and add in a percentage for profit. With e-books this is much harder. Once you've paid for the cover, edit and uploading to a retailer, and your time to write the book in the first place, there's no more cost to selling 1 copy than selling 10,000 copies. And that, right there, is why e-books are so popular with publishers!

The final, and in my view, and according to the course I went on, best method for calculating price is *value based pricing*. The value is calculated from whose perspective? Yes, that's right, the customer's. You work through three factors and allocate a value in £ to each of them:

- Revenue gains – this is about the value add of your product, what does your product give to the customer in terms of adding value.
- Cost reduction – what does your product save your customers in terms of money.
- Emotional contribution – reduced hassle, relationships, reduced risk, comfort, reliability.

OK, OK, I'm getting my marketing jargon klaxon out again!

Right, as an example, I worked with a publisher who wanted to put on a one day conference about writing GLBTQ fiction, hear from some keynote speakers in the genre, take pitches from authors, sell books, and provide an opportunity for delegates to discuss issues related to the genre.

At first they priced the tickets using the second method – cost based. They had a figure for the catering which included the venue hire, which was, say £20 and they added £5 on top as a profit.

Although this sounds reasonable it fails to take into account the value for customers of attending such an event. They get to meet their favourite authors in the genre and get copies of their books signed. They get to hear from two keynote speakers in the genre about topics relevant to the genre. Authors can pitch to the publisher and sell their own books too, as well as being able to network with readers and authors in the same genre.

If you add these elements together and try to work out a rough price, plus adding in the fact that to do all these separate things would require much driving up and down the country and time, whereas it's all put on in one place on one day, hence reducing hassle, the value is much more than simply the catering plus £5. In the end they charged about £50 and made a clear profit from the event and had a lot of very satisfied customers who felt the day represented good value.

When you consider that a book is competing for time alongside TV, radio, cinema etc, and that an average reading time of a 50,000 word novel is likely to be about three to four hours, using $0.99 as a regular pricing point is really doing a disservice to books as a whole.

If your book is set in an exotic location, you could mention it saves the customer the price of a holiday abroad so it's good value. If your book takes the reader into the past, reliving nostalgic memories, you can mention the value of reliving one's childhood memories and how your book offers a window into the past. Using other authors' reviews of your book to reassure readers that your book will be 'reliable' in that it's entertaining, emotional, nostalgic, escapist etc – supports the emotional contribution element of value based pricing.

Promotion

This is how a company promotes what it does, what its products do, to its customers. It's also called marketing communications.

Anything that communicates with your customers/readers, about your books, is marketing communications / promotion.

It includes public relations (PR), flyers/ bookmarks, exhibitions, branding, advertising, social media, using traditional media (TV, radio, magazines, newspapers) or online media (blogs, websites, e-magazines, newsletters) to talk about you, or your products to your customers.

This is the bit of marketing that gets the most air time. It is, for most people, *everything* about marketing.

Promotion shouldn't just be one-way, it should try to be a way of creating a two-way dialogue between you or your product and your customers. For instance, competitions, giveaways, involving readers in writing your work in progress. If you create a dialogue with your customer, it will feel more like a conversation and you being sociable, rather than you just handing them an advert. Remember the plumber in the dinner party before? Remember, engage engage engage, while you're promoting.

Promotions to customers should communicate your book's benefits, not simply its features. The phrase to remember is: *feature, advantage, benefit* or FAB. I'll break that down now to explain what I mean.

- Feature = the facts or characteristics of your product.
- Advantage = what the features do.

- Benefits = why customers should value the advantages. Linking your product's factual *features* to how they provide a solution – the *benefits* – for your client.
  FAB (Clarke, 2012)

I'll use a car as an example, and then move onto a book. OK, ready?

- Feature = 55 miles per gallon on combined driving cycle. (On its own, particularly for non-car people, this is basically useless.)
- Advantage = means the car uses less fuel than older models. (Now we're getting somewhere by explaining the advantage from the point of view of the customer of this feature.)
- Benefit = saves you money on fuel and road tax. (This goes further than the advantage by making the benefit very specific to the owner of the car, regardless of whether she is a car person or not.) (Jacoby, n.d.)

You can then combine all three of these into some promotional writing to communicate to your customers: *Try the new VW Golf, it gets 55 miles per gallon on the combined driving cycle. This means it uses less fuel than the previous model and will save you money on fuel and road tax.*

Let's do it for a book now. The blurb, or back cover copy, is the most obvious way a book's FAB are communicated to readers. Books, unlike cars, are less practical and more emotional products but you still have to communicate the basics so a reader knows what she's getting. And, with a book you'd be unlikely to run through FAB in that order, quite so simply as with a car. The blurb, quotes from reviews, and the strapline, are likely to be a mix of F, A and B, with slightly blurry edges between them. This doesn't matter one jot, because what's important is that when you're writing a blurb for your books you have FAB in the back of your mind and make sure you cover all three.

OK, let's have a look at what's written on a few romance books' covers and blurbs. Remember, the Benefits are from the customers' / readers' perspective, so you'd expect romance books to make a lot of the main reasons why readers enjoy romance. I will go into this in more detail in the romance chapter, but in summary, based on Janice Radway's extensive research, the main reasons why readers enjoy romance (and keep coming back for more that's similar but different) are:

1. as being compensatory (for experiences lacking in their real lives)
2. escape (in two senses of the word: escaping from their every day lives, and escaping into a fantasy world)
3. emotional experience – falling in love with the hero and experiencing the emotion of falling in love alongside the heroine. (Radway, 1991)

Example 1) *Riders* **by Jilly Cooper, 2015**

Feature: Sex and horses...Set against the glorious Cotswold countryside. A celebration of all that is most fun about being British...one of our nation's most beloved novels...

Advantage: offers an intoxicating blend of swooning romance, adventure and hilarious high jinks. Hilarious, witty, wise, astute...joyful and mischievous...Exhilarating, irresistible...

Benefit: Fun, sexy and unputdownable – a classic...a joyous experience! Settle down and have a rollicking good time. Flawlessly entertaining.

Example 2) *An Absolute Scandal* **by Penny Vincenzi, 2009**

Feature: It's the glittering eighties and [three female characters] feel happy and secure in the power and pleasure of wealth. Nothing could have prepared them for a devastating financial scandal, which turns the boom to bust.

Advantage: Twists, turns and emotional switchbacks aplenty...dazzlingly combines the old-fashioned virtues of gripping storytelling with the up-to-the-minute contemporary feel for emotional depth and insight...immersing the reader in a world of engrossing and unforgettable glamour and passion...

Benefit: Highly addictive...another absorbing page-turner...marvellously engrossing...A rampantly riveting read...

Example 3) *Deadly Sins* by Nicholas Coleridge, 2010

Feature: Two families plunged into a bitter feud of class, scandal and revenge...[male character] is the head of a lucrative multi-national PR business: he has a society wife, four presentable children...When self-made millionaire [male character] buys the land adjoining the...estate...Sex, drugs and rock 'n' roll...

Advantage: As passions run high, battles rage from boardroom to bedroom, where both wives and mistresses are coveted...in this roller coaster ride across generations and class...it is a triumph...fast fluent and beautifully observed novel...hugely entertaining...[author] drip-feeds us with one splendid set-piece after another...escapist tale ticks every sin, from pride and greed to envy, wrath and, of course, lust. A right royal romp...

Benefit: [you] will whoop with joy over the final intricately plotted pages of this wickedly funny and utterly irresistible book...guilty-pleasure reading at its naughtiest...

Example 4) *Saving Grace* by Jane Green, 2014

Feature: [heroine]...living with her husband, bestselling author [name], in a picture-perfect farmhouse on the Hudson River in New York state. Then [name] advertises for a new assistant, and [name] walks into their lives...A perfect stranger wants her perfect life...

Advantage: [heroine] is so real and so sympathetically drawn that you'll find yourself inside her skin, trapped in a situation with no way out...beautifully written, emotionally intense and psychologically fascinating portraits of people and the relationships that make up a life...A page-turner about trust, betrayal and things never being quite what they seem...

Benefit: The only escape is to keep reading...It's an emotional read...

Example 5) *Love Always* **by Harriet Evans, 2011**

Feature: Top ten bestseller...As [heroine] travels back to Cornwall for her beloved grandmother's funeral, she has no idea what fate holds in store...[heroine] has never known the truth about the tragic accident that killed her aunt...and when she finds [aunt's] diary...the past and the present start to collide.

Advantage: A powerful tale of lost love, family secrets and those little moments that can change you forever. For reading heaven read [author]...

Benefit: Escapism that brings with it the promise of 'custard yellow' sands and hot summer sun...Heart warming and hugely enjoyable...Deeply satisfying...You'll love it...Truly gripping...

You could possibly argue a case to swap some of the Benefit and Advantage elements, but that's not a productive use of time. Again, it doesn't really matter one jot. The benefit of the FAB model is that it makes you think *in a structured way* of all three elements so you can ensure you include them in your promotional materials to your readers.

A key principal of promotion is to make sure you're promoting *where your customers are*. There's no point me writing a romance book and then placing an advert in *New Scientist Magazine*, or paying for a billboard along the edge of a motorway. Although, yes, some customers may indeed read that magazine and drive a car on the motorway, it is very untargeted and will inevitably have a lot of waste.

Social media adverts use algorithms to target customers who are likely to be interested in your product. Facebook and Twitter are the best known of these. In terms of minimising waste, they are undoubtedly good. However, one of the main purposes of social media is to be social and so many users tend to ignore any promoted posts (adverts) because they're not really in the mood for being sold to and would prefer to interact and socialise with other readers and authors.

Place

This is where your customers can buy your books. It applies in terms of physical places like book shops, supermarkets etc as well as online places like Amazon, iBooks, Kobo etc. The place where your books are sold should be convenient to the customer, so don't set up a paste table in your back garden and expect your customers to all come rushing round to buy!

Place also includes how you display your books to customers. This could mean on a table at a book fair, at a conference, or on your website. Remember your website is your home online and also your shop window online. This doesn't mean you have to sell your products through your website (although you can, but I believe there are some tax issues you'd need to get over first, consult an accountant first) but can still have your book covers, blurbs, reviews on your website with buy links to online places where they can be bought – Amazon, iBooks etc.

It's likely you'll 'meet' more customers online through your website than you'll ever physically meet in person. Therefore the look, feel and usability of your website and how it represents your brand are even more important. If you were selling fruit and veg at a market stall on Tuesdays and Saturdays then you could probably do without a website. You're likely to meet all your customers in person and your physical interaction with them will make them decide whether or not to buy more fruit and veg from you.

As an author, who can sell her books to people all over the world (I'm always amused when I see my royalty statements showing customers in Australia and China, imagining them reading my books), it's much more important to have a modern, accessible, regularly updated website as your Place online.

As part of it being a modern website, it's also important to have it optimised for mobile devices. Nowadays more and more internet is browsed on the move on phones and tablets so if your website doesn't display correctly your customers may bounce right off it and onto someone else's to read their books instead. Google search puts those websites not optimised for mobile devices lower than those that are. This can mean the difference between customers finding your online Place and not.

Those 4 Ps are the core ones for the marketing mix: Product, Price, Promotion and Place.

And now I'll move onto three more reasonably recent additions that originally came from the service industry but are felt to be equally important to other marketing decisions.

People

Have you ever taken a product back to the shop where you bought it to complain and explained to customer services what went wrong and what you want them (the company) to do to resolve it? Or maybe you've phoned a call centre to complain about a product or service like insurance or broadband etc?

Even though the individual you're talking to is very unlikely to have had anything to do with selling or promoting or making the product in question, you are taking them to 'be' the company. This P for People means that people are effectively representing the company.

When you meet editors from publishing houses at conferences, notice how they are dressed in a way that feels appropriate to the publisher. Are romance publisher editors likely to be wearing torn jeans, ripped T-shirts showing their midriff and metal piercings through their tongue and belly button? No, they'll probably wear business attire, a lanyard with their name and publisher role. They may have a sash with the publisher's name on it in a nod and wink to beauty pageants. They may even be dressed up as their favourite heroine or hero from romantic fiction.

Notice how they speak about the publisher. Do they say they're terrible to work for and that they never get back to authors? Do they say they're paid terribly and they hate the books they publish? No. Of course they don't.

How do these editors and other people you met, behave on social media? Do they complain about their employer? Do they say they hate romantic fiction and prefer reading literary fiction or non-fiction instead, but this is only a job? Of course not.

The editors *are*, to all intents and purposes 'The Publisher' at the conference. They are representing the publisher and so their behaviour, appearance, discussions, all have to be congruent with the publisher's brand and identity.

There are other aspects to People including after-sales support and support to the most popular products, but as most authors don't directly sell books to their customers – instead using a third party vendor like Amazon – this isn't applicable.

However, as an author, *you are your brand*. You are representing your products, your books, the things your customers spend their hard earned money on. While still being yourself, you should, when appearing in public (in person at conferences etc and online) ensure you represent your brand, your books, yourself positively. This comes back to my earlier point about social media.

Marian Keyes has a wonderful Twitter persona. She tweets about family, friends, books, cakes, TV, and keeps it upbeat and positive – much like her books really. She steers well clear of politics and religion to avoid alienating her readers and stays 'on brand' with her online interactions. She's the same on TV interviews and online videos she's posted. She talks about her mental health and alcohol and drug addiction issues openly and honestly and it is at times quite moving. However, that's also congruent with her brand and her books (that often include descriptions of mental ill health and substance addiction).

Physical evidence

This is particularly important for services that customers can't see, or when a customer is trying a new product from a new source for the first time. Customers will check online for Physical Evidence to confirm that the new product is a good bet, or not.

A well organised, tidy website homepage is reassuring to a new customer.

The Physical Evidence should confirm what sort of product the customer is about to buy from you. If you write feel-good sagas set in the fifties and sixties, having a website and social media feed filled with pictures of devils, skulls and guns won't engender you to many customers.

Conversely, if you write about the occult and life after death, having a website full of pictures of pretty shoes, dresses and flowers will confuse customers.

Again, the watchword here, is congruence.

Reviews are Physical Evidence of what other customers felt about your products. Adding review quotes to your book covers, posting positive reviews on your website and on social media, are all ways to reassure customers about your products. The views of other customers (they don't have to be from review websites or official reviewers) are a powerful way to support your customers to buy your books with confidence.

Taking the previous point one step further, if you can support a place online or in person, where your customers can talk to others about your books, that makes the above point interactive. This can be done through 'street team' which are private groups on Facebook for your fans. In addition, asking customers to record a short video about what they loved about your book and uploading that to your website and social media is much more powerful than simply a written review. Because these discussions and reviews aren't coming from yourself or anyone you're paying to be positive (don't even think about it, you will get found out, trust me. And don't think about posing as other social media profiles and posting great reviews about your own work. It always gets found out) it means customers will be much more likely to believe it than simply an advert. This sort of communication of customer-to-customer feedback about your books is called *word of mouth*.

Word of mouth is worth its weight in gold.

Process

Have you heard of the 'customer journey'? Marketing jargon klaxon!

This is basically the whole time from first interacting with the company to the moment you take delivery of your product and it also extends to after-sales support. I'm going to use a purchase of a car as an example because it should be something most people should be familiar with.

The customer journey starts when you arrive at the garage. The salesman asks you how he can help you and then asks you a series of questions about what you're looking for from a car. Do you do long journeys in it? How many people does it need to seat? How important is fuel economy? Are you interested in its speed and handling? How important is its luggage capacity? What is your budget?

Then he shows you a few different cars that should provide a transport solution to the questions you've asked. He asks if you'd like to sit in the vehicle, open the doors, ask any questions about it. When you find a car you like the look of he asks if you'd like to have a test drive. During the test drive he explains more features, their advantage and benefits to you as the potential customer. He asks how you think this vehicle would meet your needs.

You decide that is the car for you so you then discuss pricing, payment options, guarantee, warranty etc. You discuss timing for when you can pick it up and he gives you a number to call if there are any problems after you've bought the new vehicle.

Although, as authors, you're unlikely to be selling products direct to customers, you may be selling manuscript appraisals, writing retreat places, workshop places etc. You need to ensure that however the customers interact with you, it's easy. If a customer emails you, make sure you reply to them. If you have a phone message, call the person back.

If you've run a giveaway of a book, contact the person who won and send them the book they've won, promptly.

If you're sending out ARCs of your books, asking readers to post reviews, be clear where you'd like them to post the reviews. Explain how you'd like them to let you know if they're unable to post a review. Be clear if you have a process if they didn't like your book – would you prefer they don't post the review, or email you first with it? Make it easy for others to interact with you.

Imagine calling a bank and being asked to pick from six different, eight button menus before being plunged into a dark telephonic abyss. Don't be that hard to interact with.

One final word on the 7 Ps of the marketing mix
You have to consider all of the elements. Often people focus on the Promotion element, because they think that's all there is to marketing. You can't just think about the Product or the Price or the Promotion, and ignore the other elements. Some elements are more important and more applicable to

books than others, as I've explained above. But it's important to logically work through each of the 7 elements.

Things to remember
- Marketing mix – a framework of P factors (Product, Price, Promotion, Place, People, Physical Evidence, Process) to go through for each book when considering how to market it.
- Marketing communications – anything that communicates with your customers about your book.
- Differentiate – spelling out why your book is different, and by implication better, than other similar ones.
- Relationship marketing – developing an ongoing relationship with your readers, encouraging them to come back to you for future books, rather than focussing on one single sale. Newsletters, asking for reviews through giving out ARCs, involving readers while writing your stories, are all ways to engage engage engage readers and develop ongoing relationships.
- Feature advantage benefit – FAB – a framework to think about how to write book blurbs, anything that communicates about your book to customers.
- Word of mouth – readers talking to other readers about how much they love your books. Much more likely to be believed than an author telling readers how great their own book is. Use customer reviews to communicate this to other readers.

Things to consider
- How can you differentiate your books from others in a similar or the same genre?
- Go through the FAB model for one of your own books and imagine writing the book cover quotes.

Things to do
- Work through the marketing mix (four or seven factors however many you think relevant) for your latest book

release. If you don't know the answers to some of the questions, ask your publisher. If you self published it, ask yourself if you consciously considered each of these factors. Are there any gaps you don't know the answer to?

• Look at your four and five star reviews, are you sharing these with other readers? Think about a way to share them with other readers that you feel comfortable with. Remember, it's not you saying those things about your books, it's other customers; you're just bringing it to other readers' attention.

CHAPTER 4 - What marketing includes and why you should be doing all of it – Part 1

Marketing is so much more than just promotion, so I have two chapters covering this. Chapter 4 and Chapter 5 include a lot of probably new-to-you terms and marketing jargon which I'll explain and illustrate using examples. Ready?

Marketing research

All marketing decisions should be taken on the basis of evidence and we get the evidence from research. This includes online surveys, focus groups, phone surveys, in person surveys and polls.

As authors you can do any of these if you have the time, inclination and money. You don't have to pay marketing research companies, or marketing consultants to do this for you.

There are two main types of research: quantitative and qualitative.

Qualitative research is about the qualities, the open questions, the 'how did it feel?' the 'how was it for you?' the 'what did you think?' the 'what did you want to be changed?' sort of questions. With this you're looking for common themes, similar comments and once you have numbers of 20 or more you can start looking for patterns. Trying to analyse for patterns with three or four responses is pretty pointless.

Quantitative research is about the numbers – how would you rate the book out of five stars? Out of these three factors which would you rate as the most important to buying a romance book? Out of these genres in romance which are your favourite? How many romance books do you buy in an average month? Which of these price points would you think is reasonable for a 50,000 word book?

With these you need high numbers of responses to be able to draw confident conclusions from the data. That's about whether it's statistically significant and I'm not going to say any more about that here. If you *really* want to understand about statistical significance, I suggest you read the reams about it online.

Next time you're with some customers, ask them informal questions about what they like to read, why, what they thought about one of your books, what they think you could do to make them better. And hey presto, you've just run a loose informal focus group!

If you have an email list of customers, you could send them an online survey – Surveymonkey is free up to a certain number of questions and there are other free online survey tools available.

Data collection
There are two types of data you collect during marketing research: primary data and secondary data.

Primary data is what you collect yourself by doing your own research – asking your own questions, sending your own surveys etc. It's essentially new data you've collected.

Secondary data is, by contrast, data that already exists. It can be in the form of reviews of your books (both qualitative in terms of the words readers say and quantitative in terms of the star ratings they give). People talk about doing 'desk research' and this is just a fancy term for spending some time online Googling stuff in a targeted strategic way, which is collecting secondary data.

When conducting research you should be clear what your objective of conducting it is. And make sure that all the research you do, primary and secondary data and collecting qualitative and quantitative data, all feeds back to your main objective. Marketing jargon klaxon!

Now, that probably sounds like lots of marketing jargon, so I'll use an example from the publishing world.

I was asked to produce a marketing plan for a publisher who wanted to increase their discoverability within their genre of romance.

Guess where I started the marketing plan?

No, I didn't just write a plan for them, I conducted some research to inform my decisions.

I researched other publishers' websites to find out how they took submissions, their book pricing, the genres they published, the types of covers their books had. This was secondary data as it was all there floating about on the internet.

I researched customer reviews for the publisher's books drawing out themes from the comments in terms of what customers liked and areas for improvement. Again, more secondary data.

I researched authors in that genre, asking some questions about what support their publishers provided them (to give the client publisher an idea of what they were up against and how they could improve their offer). This was primary data of both quantitative and qualitative nature.

Let's look at another example of research you could do as an author.

1. You want to pitch your next book idea to your publisher (or you're trying to decide what to write next if you're self publishing). You make yourself a nice cup of tea or coffee then spend five minutes or so to look at the bestselling books in the romance genre over the past three to six months, in the sub genre that's similar to what you currently write (erotica / contemporary / humour / historical etc).

2. Take another five minutes or so to analyse their titles, trying to see if there are any similarities in them.

3. Get another cup of tea or coffee now, you've earned it, and then spend about an hour, or if you can't bear it, just half an hour to pick one of these books and look at 30 of the five star reviews on Amazon and analyse for similar topics, themes, comments to find out what really turned readers on to that book.

4. More tea or coffee, then with the same book, spend another half an hour to read 30 (or at least double figures if there's not that many) of the one and two star reviews on Amazon and analyse for similar themes, topics, comments to find out what really annoyed and turned off some readers.

5. Make a note of the price at which the book is being sold on Amazon (keep the format consistent so you're not comparing e-book with paperback or hardback). This information is for you, so a quick note of prices is fine. It's about looking at average prices for comparable books to yours.

6. More tea or coffee, then spend half an hour to make notes about the cover – colours, sorts of images, straplines used, any additional promo offer stickers on the covers (competitions, winning prizes etc). If it's easier, you could just save copies of these covers.

7. That will probably be enough for one day for most people, but if you're really enjoying this, feel free to fill your boots and you can repeat steps three to six with five or more books and other authors in a similar sub genre. If you've had enough, take a break. Read a romance novel. Have a bath. But come back to this tomorrow and repeat steps three to six as described above.

8. You should have been making notes as you've been working through this list, drinking tea and coffee. If not, spend twenty to thirty minutes writing these findings, heading by heading (use the numbers in this list) into a summary, covering information on points four to six across all

the books you looked at and after each section write yourself some conclusions about what this means for you. This is where you're moving on from raw data and information to *insight*. Insight is where you're drawing conclusions from the data and applying them to your own books. No one is going to mark this. You don't need to show this to anyone else. This is you using the data you've found to look for patterns, similarities, differences, so you can then think, 'I want to replicate this!' or 'I like what they've done there, I'm going to adapt that, be inspired by it, avoid reinventing any wheels!'

9. Use these insights and your own conclusions to steer the details of your next book or proposal. Remember, romance is a popular, customer-led genre, so there's no shame in thinking this way. Rest assured, publishers do, because they're all about the money, and being an author thinking that way can only improve your chances of sales, publication, getting agented (in the romance genre).

Speaking from experience, I did this after my first four books were published. They were critically evaluating well with review websites and from people who understood it, but from wider romance readers they seemed to be somewhat missing the point. They criticised the lack of a strong romance at the heart, they wanted more adult exploration of on-page sensual content, they wanted to understand the other character's motivations which was impossible in my first person narrative, and they wanted a more likeable hero if they were going to spend the whole book with him. Basically I realised I wasn't really writing male male romance I was writing gay fiction with a dash of romance and lots of humour and camp. In short, male male romance readers were opening a box of cornflakes to find a couple of salmon!

I abandoned my first person coming of age, wider than romance, questionable main character concepts of old and wrote an all-out male male romance. It focussed on the development of the two men's romance, both characters were likeable (or at least liveable), there was more on page sensual scenes as part of the plot and character development (I dislike intensely sex for the sake of sex in books it makes me yawn and skim read, but any more of that's not for now), and it was in third person point of view alternate chapters between the two main characters' viewpoint. That next book received much better reviews and sales.

Was I writing to a formula? I don't think so.

Was I compromising my artistic credentials? I don't think I have any... I just sit down to tell an entertaining story!

At the end of the day, they were *my* characters, in *my* setting, with *my* romance at its core. I just bore in mind the customer feedback to make this story more commercial and marketable than before. My first few books were just for me and I didn't know or care anything about the market then.

Marketing audit

I'm sure you've heard of a PESTEL analysis? If not, no matter, it's a list of things to systematically take you through looking at the wider context in which you're selling your books.

You should, in turn, work through the elements of the PESTEL analysis. It doesn't matter which order you go through these elements, just that you take some time to think about each of them, one at a time.

I'll go through each one with examples of the things you need to think about in relation to books and publishing. As with most of these tools it's best not to get too hung up about whether something goes under one category or the other. It's more important to use the tool to systematically think in a very broad way about the external factors affecting books and publishing, that is, the world in which you're selling your books.

Political – significant political changes in the world stage will affect people's buying habits and taste. I read there's a significant amount of Brexit fan fiction now! The political climate affects satire and entertainment, do you want to reflect that in your fiction, or do you want to provide a blissfully ignorant escape from it? Neither answer is right, but it's something worth considering when you're promoting your book. Is your book an antidote to politics or a way of mocking it, or a way of holding a mirror to it in an up to date way? Has the Office of Fair Trading changed anything in relation to pricing of books? They made it legal to sell books at different prices from their cover price many years ago.

Economic – a recession or an economic boom time will affect how people can and want to spend their money. It will affect how much disposable income they have and how much discretionary spending is used on items such as entertainment (of which books are included). The exchange rates between the UK and US will affect pricing of books. Is the cost of paper changing, which will affect book prices? With bookshops closing regularly and many consumers buying their books while picking up their weekly groceries, what is the future of book launches in shops? Spending being down on big home purchases like new houses, sofas, while being up on small affordable luxuries like lipsticks, are an indication people are pulling their horns in spending-wise and that we could be in for a recession.

Social – changes in demographics of readers getting used to reading short pieces on their devices may affect the appetite for short bite-sized fiction to read on a commute or in a lunch break at work. There is now a generation of consumers who don't know a world before the internet existed. This generation is used to everything they read on their devices being free (because the internet is free right?) So how does that fit with e-books? What are the social trends on customers' spending on books related to previous years? If it's gone down how do you make sure your books are the must-have products for that year? Social trends also affect the content of books – noir thrillers with female leads, sex and control books in light of *50 Shades of Grey*, the popularity of the *Great British Bake Off* led to a whole host of baking themed books. What is the current trend, or the next one that's nascent, and do you want to write something linked or inspired by it so you're at the start of the next wave?

Technological – the introduction of tablets and smart phones and using them as reading devices rather than a stand-alone e-reader (Kindle etc). With apps on other devices is the Kindle dead? Does this mean more people can have access and are likely to buy e-books than before, or fewer because of the social aspects above? Print on demand changed self-publishing significantly; it meant that if you wanted to self publish a paperback you didn't have to risk numbers and order thousands at a time. With self-publishing possible for anyone with a computer and internet connection, where is the value added aspect of a traditional publishing deal?

Environmental – is the fact that books are made of paper a concern to consumers? Are e-books perceived to be more environmentally friendly? What can you do in terms of sustainable paper sourcing for paperbacks?

Legal – having to pay VAT in the UK on e-books but not on physical books – this would affect your pricing considerations. E-books bring about the risk of illegal piracy (unlike paperbacks). What would your stance be when finding your e-books on these websites?

Marketing communications
Marketing jargon klaxon!
This is just a fancy marketing word for anything that communicates about your book with a customer. It is the Promotion in the marketing mix we've already covered.

In terms of books' marketing communications, this includes:

- book covers (packaging)
- the blurb (what is written on the back of the book cover, or in an e-book's description)
- reviews – when you quote them on book covers, your blog or social media you're using them to communicate what other customers loved about your book. Obviously you don't want to communicate bad reviews because you wouldn't expect a book cover to have a quote that said, 'I hated it!' or a flyer printed that says '1* didn't finish' now would you?
- an author's website and blog
- sales promotion – discounted pricing, money off your next purchase, multi packs (three for the price of two), free samples, limited editions (new covers, additional chapters, interviews with the author), competitions and prize draws.
- sponsorship – at a conference I helped organise, a few big names in the genre sponsored items such as swag bags, lanyards, the booklet. This meant their name was all over the event on these items. It's a more unconscious way of promoting yourself, a bit like the *Michelin Restaurant Guide*. You're hoping that by putting your name in their mind over a period of time when they're wondering who to read next, miraculously your name will pop into their head.
- flyers, bookmarks, pens, notepads etc – best to make these something that lasts longer than a coffee and won't end up in the bin as soon as the person's left, so items that are useful like pens and notepads are better than simply flyers. Also better to have them promoting yourself as an author pointing to your website (that you can then update with your latest books) rather than just your latest book because that will soon not be your latest book and you'll have to get another load printed.
- social media posts mentioning your book

- personal selling – sitting at a table selling your books
- adverts (in print media like magazines, bookshop windows, newspapers, online like Facebook or Twitter promoted posts)
- public relations (PR) – this pretends to be an article in a magazine or newspaper or online, but really it's simply a way to promote your book and tell customers how great it is. Now so much media is online you don't need a publicist to do your own PR! The key to something being PR and not just an advert is *there needs to be a story*. Woman publishes new book is not a story. Woman finds mother's memoirs in attic and uses them as the basis of a book she's published – that's a story! Try to think about it from the magazine's point of view (and I include online magazines too such as blogs and review websites etc). What can you give them to fill their pages that's more than simply 'buy my book it's just out'? When you write a guest blog post try to include an interesting story about yourself, your book, your characters, and then at the end link back to the book and its blurb and cover. After all, you're an author so coming up with a story angle linked to your book can't be too hard, right? The key element to remember when you're trying to get a magazine etc interested in your story is to include: who, what, where, why, when, how. Covering all of those, making sure there's an actual story to tell and not simply 'I've written a book' and starting with the most important bit will make you head and shoulders above everyone else who's trying to promote their book in this way. If you think of it like simply telling friends how you wrote the book, what happened along the way, the story behind the story, rather than trying to sell, you're half way there already.

Clever marketing communications don't just tell your customers about the product; they should be there to engage customers intellectually. That probably sounds really esoteric and intellectual. OK, so have you ever watched an advert and smiled or laughed, or wanted to tell someone about it? I bet you have. Once, I watched a TV ad and cried because it looked like a great TV drama I'd love to watch; it was an advert for a bank, using nostalgia and family to reassure its customers of how strong it is. I was livid!

One of my favourite adverts is, surprise surprise, a car advert from the eighties. I've always loved cars, Mum and Dad have owned VW cars basically forever. And the particular Golf in the advert was the same as Dad's which always makes me smile even now, although he's not alive. The advert is for the VW Golf, and it shows a woman who's just left her husband, walking down the street. She hangs her fur coat on a lamp post, drops her diamond wedding ring through the letter box, removes her pearl necklace (it was the eighties) and throws it into a bin, she throws her silver brooch into a bush, and she's just about to drop the keys of her car down the drain too, when she thinks again. She continues walking along the road until she reaches her car, unlocks it with the key and gets in, tapping the steering wheel and smiling before pulling off and driving into the distance. The text at the end reads 'If only everything in life was as reliable as a VW.' (VW, 1987)

So, how do you make your book adverts clever? I'm assuming that like me, you don't have the same budget as VW to promote your books, well anyway, there's plenty of ways you can make interesting marketing communications for your customers. At its most basic level you need to ensure all your marketing communications DRIP.

Yes, yes, yes, I too hear another marketing jargon klaxon! This one's very simple to explain:

- Differentiate
- Reinforce
- Inform
- Persuade

And I'll explain how you can use this for your books now.

Differentiate – how does your book stand out from all the other books with similar covers, pretty similar blurbs and similar basic storylines? Why should I buy your book rather than all the others? Here are some examples:

'...giving Jackie Collins a run for her money' That's Life (Victoria Fox *Wicked Ambition*)

'Treat yourself to a Vincenzi' (written in a bow tied up around the middle of the book cover)

'Adele Parks' novels are a fabulous mix of comedy, real life and emotional depth.' Daily Express (*About last Night*)

'The wig-flushing scene is outasight. Susann didn't become the queen of girl trash for nothing.' Janet Fitch, author of White Oleander (*Valley of the Dolls*)

'Green is women's fiction royalty...a compelling family drama' Glamour (*The Patchwork Marriage*)

'[Trollope] has the knack of rendering people's lives with infinite clarity and truth...This is no Brady Bunch, but the emotionally messy world of children (and adults) is so palpably real that the reader will know them as well or better than their own children.' Library Journal (*Other People's Children*)

Reinforce – this is about consolidating and strengthening previous messages and experiences related to your books. Here are some examples:

'Some people are beginning to measure out their lives in terms of the next Joanna Trollope...' (*A Spanish Lover*)

'The hottest young female writer in Britain and the voice of a generation' Mirror (*Sushi for Beginners*)

'Reading Penny Vincenzi is an addictive experience' Elizabeth Buchan (*Into Temptation*)

'Irresistible...I devoured it in a day...she's on cracking form...just read it and enjoy' Sunday Telegraph (*The Man Who Made Husbands Jealous*)

'The most successful novelist on Planet Earth.' Washington Post (*Dance to the Piper* by Nora Roberts)

Inform – this is about making the book's content, plot, characters, setting known to the reader. This is simply factual information so a reader who enjoys sagas set in Victorian era doesn't accidentally pick up a contemporary bonkbuster. The basic features such as the word count or page number could be included here, but generally books don't include information about this except in the description alongside the publisher. Readers aren't as interested in these basic features in a book, as say a car. This element is basically the same as the F part of *Feature* Advantage Benefit (FAB) we discussed earlier.

Persuade – this is to encourage the reader to purchase, by sharing positive aspects of the book that will *persuade* her to *buy*. The important thing with this is that it's based on what will persuade the sort of readers who enjoy that type of book to buy it. There's no point trying to persuade a crime lover to buy a category romance by adding something about a who-done-it on the cover. Chances are they'll have passed it by because of the book cover anyway. This is all about persuading the customers *who are interested in that type of book* to buy yours, above all the others. That probably sounds quite esoteric, so how about some examples:

'Read Joanna Trollope's *Other People's Children*...You won't be sorry you did.' USA Today

'Greed. Lust. Power. It's dangerous at the top.' (*Wicked Ambition* by Victoria Fox)

'Just too exciting to put down' Closer (ibid)

'Gripping and emotional' Star (*The Patchwork Marriage*)

'Beautifully written, warm and romantic...the perfect holiday read' Rachel Hore, author of A *Gathering Storm* (*Return to Mandalay*)

'Vividly written with a compelling storyline, this is top escapism' Closer (ibid)

'I love Kate Reddy...her tale made me cry twice, and laugh often' Independent on Sunday (*I don't Know How She Does It* by Allison Pearson)

'A tantalising novel packed with power struggles, greed and sex. This is Collins at her finest' Closer (*The Power Trip* by Jackie Collins)

Are adverts worth it?

Adverts are also marketing communications and they too should DRIP. However, the most important things to understand about adverts are:

1) they're never as trusted as word of mouth from other readers or public relations content. An advert is automatically more suspicious to readers because they know it's an advert and for some that makes them put up their guards. They instinctively mistrust advertisers because they're perceived to be telling lies. Other readers on the other hand are honest, so other readers' reviews are much more trusted. Hence, try to quote them in your adverts. Also PR is often not known to be PR. If a reader enjoys an interview with you about your latest book and how you came to that idea, they're simply viewing it as a nice piece of free content. And if you tack on a 'by the way this book is out now' at the end, they're kind of warmed up to you and are more likely to take action than if they were simply reading an advert saying 'by the way this book is out now'.

2) they need to be engaging and have a Call To Action (CTA). This is asking them to do something as a result of seeing the advert. Download a sample. Buy now while it's at

99p. Enter a competition to win your back catalogue etc. If there's no call to action they'll see the advert and simply move on with their lives afterwards. Adverts should be engaging, not simply something we can ignore during our busy day. Make your advert engaging by asking the reader to do something.

3) need to be clear what the main purpose of your advert is. If it's selling books then because it's on social media, it's not always the right place to sell. Remember the dinner party analogy earlier? However, if you base your advert on a quote from another reader, include some engaging content your readers will like – a picture of a hunky man, reference to a dancing competition, a picture of a glamorous holiday location – the advert then becomes more about the reader than about you, which is what you should aim for. (Vahl, 2014)

However, all is not lost with social media ads and promoted posts.

Even though Facebook may not be the best place to actually sell, it's a great place to increase engagement with you, your website and build your email list (for use later with newsletters etc and other relationship marketing good stuff to then sell books).

Facebook ads are great for targeting a specific type of reader. More on segmenting, targeting and positioning in the next section, but for now I'll give an example. Say you were interested in targeting women aged 34 – 55 who enjoyed romance books, European holiday destinations and baking, Facebook could find you those women. Unlike Google Adwords, on Facebook you can't specify 'buying' words. For example, if someone's Googling 'best romance books set in Italy' you know they're looking to buy a romance book set in Italy. However, with Facebook ads you can't specify in the targeting that you want people who are looking to buy anything.

Can you see why Facebook ads aren't necessarily great for making people buy books? It comes back to my *social media* point earlier.

Unlike doing a Google search, when someone's on Facebook they're not looking to buy something, they're more likely looking to interact and talk about something, and connect with others with similar interests.

However, Facebook ads do allow you to target readers who enjoy similar genre books to yours, who like other author and publisher pages that produce books similar to yours. Again, this is just homing in on the specific target of reader you're wanting to reach.

Facebook is mainly a social media resource and social media experts recommend focusing about 20% of your budget on building an audience (liking your page) or getting engagement through boosted normal Facebook posts, 70% budget on adding people to your email list (to develop a relationship with them and sell through a newsletter etc afterwards) and only 10% of the budget on trying to get actual sales. (Bernazzi, 2016)

What can you do to make your Facebook ads stand a better chance of working (within the parameters I've explained above)?

1) **Make it visual.** How often have you written a big long Facebook post and then got no responses? What about if you write the post and also include a picture? I bet that gets loads more comments and shares?

Facebook is a very visual social media and because there's no restriction on post length (unlike Twitter) you have the space to include a visual. A picture of a book cover, or a sample of the book at a high drama scene, some review quotes from other readers – these can all be made visually appealing pictures.

Think about including a short video. A picture of something related to the theme of your books (a gas mask, a cupcake, a beach and the sea).

Pictures should be more creative than simply the cover (the cover is also fine by the way). Think of pictures of things that sum up the themes / emotion / setting of your book. Pick three to five items, or a sunset, or a building that readers see in your book. Take the readers to the Greek island you're writing about. Remember, romance is about escape. Let your advert show them a window into the world you've created that they can escape into. If you want to promote not just one book, but your whole brand, type of books, include multiple book covers, multiple review quotes / extracts and emphasise that you're more than a one book author. By engaging with you, they'll have lots of books to enjoy. Be careful which images you use to promote your books in this way. You can't just pick an image from a Google search and use it to promote a book due to copyright. There are plenty of websites with images that can be used in this way. Better to be safe than sorry.

2) **Make it relevant.** You'll be paying every time a reader clicks on your advert. Make sure your advert reflects their values / wants / needs / interests. There's nothing more irritating than being sold a book about sci-fi dystopia when you only read romances set in the 1950s.

3) **Have a tempting value proposition or 'why should I care' statement that appeals to the readers.** This may be 50% off the price. It may be 'free e-book'. Also, remember DRIP – this is where you should include statements covering those elements about your book. These can be quotes from other readers, statements of your own about your book, but make sure they do at least one of the four DRIP elements. Don't lie either. Don't say your books are loved all around the world by

countless readers if it's your first and you've only sold it in the UK.

4) **Give it a clear 'call to action' – CTA.** Something the reader has to do. If the sale ends in a week, they have a deadline to download the book or sign up to the newsletter. Ask the reader to do something in response to your advert. Remember don't advertise, instead engage, engage, engage! (Bernazzi, 2016)

Things to remember
• Research – all decisions made about marketing should be based on evidence and a way to gather evidence is to carry out research. This can be done through gathering numbers – quantitative data, or opinions, themes, topics – qualitative data. As well as gathering new data by talking to your customers etc, you can also use the wealth of information already available online in reviews, industry data reports etc.
• PESTEL – a framework to support thinking about the wider environment in which you're writing and publishing your book.
• DRIP – make sure every time you communicate about your books to your customers (flyers, book covers, blog posts, back copy blurb etc) you do one of the four things from DRIP: differentiate, reinforce, inform, persuade.
• CTA – call to action – make sure every time you communicate with your customers you're asking them to do something. Download a free sample, buy the book, read other reviews, tell you if they're enjoying your book...

Things to Consider
• Have you ever done any desk research by looking at your own book reviews? Are there any patterns and themes you can pick out to influence how or what you write next?
• What do you think will be the biggest PESTEL change in the next five years to influence books?

- Look at some adverts for anything – a car, a supermarket, a book – and try to pick out which part or parts of DRIP they're doing?

Things to do

- Pick your favourite romance book ever and look at customer reviews online. Analyse the comments for common themes, topics, similar ideas about why readers love that book.

- Research online for some romance book industry reports and familiarise yourself with them; is there anything in terms of trends you can learn from, or maybe it's about book pricing if you self publish?

- After doing these two earlier steps, write a brief report summarising your findings and include some recommendation for how to do things differently. Imagine you are writing the report for someone else so the changes you're proposing must be clear and based on the evidence you've collected.

- Have a cup of tea or coffee, or a large glass of wine, and rest before reading the next chapter.

CHAPTER 5 - What marketing includes and why you should be doing all of it – Part 2

As I said, marketing is a deep and wide subject. In its broadest sense, it should be something you're always thinking about when writing, so we're coming back to all the elements that it includes, and why they're relevant to you, a romance author.

STP – Segmenting, Targeting and Positioning audiences

Coming back to what marketing includes, we now move onto STP.

Massive marketing jargon klaxon! OK, I'll break these terms down and explain each of them, one at a time.

Segmenting means dividing up your customers into groups with similar characteristics. The important thing to understand here is it's based on the consumers' needs wants, characteristics, rather than the products. You first identify different consumer groups, their different wants, and then develop your products to match them.

Car manufacturers do this with their new cars. There are now many more different segments of cars than there were 30 years ago. There used to be supermini, small family car, large family car, luxury car, sports car. Now there are all of those plus sub-supermini, off-roader, people carrier, luxury supermini etc. Before developing a new car, manufacturers work out the different segments of customers, what their specific needs are, and then develop a car to meet those needs.

Traditionally the publishing industry didn't work like this – why would it, it's about art isn't it? The Harlequin model of book publishing 'changed significantly from that of locating or even creating an audience for an existing manuscript to that of locating or creating a manuscript for an already-constituted reading public.' (Radway, 1991, p43) There are still parts of the publishing industry that operate more like the former model, but genre publishing is all based on the latter model. Editors and publishers know that books similar to x and y will appeal to readers, so they want more of the same but different to x and y books to sell to their readers.

Trying to market a book to *everybody* means it will appeal to *nobody*.

When your editor or publisher asks what your next story is like, is it like a Jackie Collins set in post war Liverpool? Think about any product, they're almost always divided into different types of customer. Take toothpaste – there's whitening, sensitive, fluoride protection, children's, travel packs etc. If a manufacturer only sells one type of toothpaste they're trying to put all their eggs (or toothpaste) in one basket. By segmenting their customers into different groups with similar requirements, they can then sell a whole range of products, rather than just one type of that product.

There are many different ways of segmenting customers, including age, income or socio-economic background, ethnicity, type of media consumed. You would tend to pick a way to segment your customers *based on characteristics that link back to your product*. For example if you were trying to segment for a new car you probably wouldn't segment based on the type of media they consumed, you'd be more likely to segment on the basis of age, income, number of children, hobbies, beliefs and values, life stage, types of holiday taken etc.

Similarly with books you can segment the customers based on age, gender, interests and hobbies, marital status etc.

And once you've decided on what basis you're going to segment your customers, to pick out one particular type of customer, you can then divide them again into a smaller segment. Take fiction readers for example. Once you've split it between fiction and non-fiction, then you can divide between the main genres of fiction: romance, action adventure, sci-fi, fantasy, speculative fiction, suspense/ thriller, young adult, new adult, horror, mystery, historical, women's fiction, literary fiction, family sagas etc. (Patterson, 2016)

Let's assume you've picked romance, because you're a romance author that's probably what you're most interested in. Within romance you could include both category romances (where romance is the main story) family sagas and women's fiction, and within those three genres you can then segment into different customer requirements.

The best book example of segmenting, targeting and positioning (that's what the T and P stand for by the way) is Mills and Boon's category romances. Rather than trying to sell romances to everyone who likes romances they've segmented their offer into categories based on different customer tastes. It's really no different from providing a people carrier for customers who want to transport seven children and a sports car for people who want to drive fast.

This approach for romance uses a marketing mindset (used by manufacturers of cars, toothpaste, TVs etc for years) and applies it to art. Janice Radway in her book, *Reading the Romance* describes it: 'Harlequin operates on the assumption that a book can be marketed like a can of beans or a soap powder. Its extraordinary profit figures convincingly demonstrate that books do not necessarily have to be thought of and marketed as unique objects but can be sold regularly and repetitively to a permanent audience on the basis of brand-name identification alone.' (Radway 1991, p39)

Remember my point about the brand of an author, but that sometimes it can be the publisher. In the case of Mills and Boon, the publisher is the brand rather than the author. Readers come back time and time again for similar but different books from the same romance line. It's no coincidence that Harlequin hired a self-described 'soap salesman' Heisey from Proctor and Gamble in 1971 to develop their marketing strategy. Heisey researched romance readers' motivations for reading and their preferences for character and plot so these could all be incorporated in their marketing communications. (Radway, 1991) The advertising campaigns featured the publisher's name more prominently than the author's name or book title which cut advertising costs due to standardisation.

Mills and Boon currently offers nine different categories of romance, ranging from historical, supernatural through modern and sweet to passionate and set in a medical setting. Here Mills and Boon has segmented the readers of romance into nine different very specific categories: Modern, Historical, Medical, True Love, Desire, Heroes, Supernatural, HQ and Dare series.

And then we come onto the T – targeting.

Targeting means looking at how potentially commercially attractive each of the segments is. Say you've segmented fiction buyers by type of fiction they read including the long list of fiction types I've already mentioned. As a romance author you're probably only going to be interested in looking at people who like to buy romance. There's not much point in targeting crime or sci-fi readers if you write romance. Once you've identified the most commercially attractive segment (based on previous sales, based on a gap in the market, based on research with customers) then you pick this segment to target. Let's go back to Harlequin for another example of this.

When they started publishing they printed all sorts including mysteries, Westerns, cooking books as well as the romances it bought from the British Mills and Boon. Based on purely sales figures Harlequin worked out that the romance books were selling exceptionally well and better than the other categories. Without even trying, they'd found out that romance buyers were a more profitable segment of book buyers than others. Since then, this has been proved by research about book buyers and their buying habits.

Around about this time 'publishing executives discovered that three-fifths of the American book-reading public was composed of women under fifty' and reports at the time related to the 'extraordinary success being enjoyed by the "contemporary romances with exotic settings" produced by...Harlequin Enterprises.' (Radway, 1991, p41) Mills and Boon then targeted these customers and changed their books to better meet their needs. This is backed up by the research they conducted with customers asking them what their favourite settings, characters, and storylines were to ensure their romance exactly met their customers' needs. They must be getting something right because worldwide Harlequin sells over 130,000,000 books which is about four books per second. (Harlequin website, n.d.)

Positioning – and now we come onto the final letter from the STP framework. Positioning is basically a fancy marketing way to say tailoring what your product offers to best meet the group of people (segment) you're trying to sell to, as well as developing a marketing mix (Product, Price, Promotion, Place etc) to best work with that segment of customers and your product.

So how do you do that with a book? Marketing professionals like a diagram or a map, so as ever we like to map out the market for the products you're talking about.

Imagine the below boxes are like a graph with the x horizontal axis representing how much sexual content a book has, ranging from the far left being complete fade-to-black, through sweet light descriptions focussing on the emotions and to the far right being explicit nuts and bolts detail like you'd get in erotica.

Now imagine the y vertical axis, from top to bottom of the page, represents the glamour of the location of the book, ranging from *cosy* at the bottom of the page, through to *international jet setting locations* at the top of the page.

You could pick any two factors to go on these axes that you're most interested in mapping, related to books – realism of characters, time period, strength of happy ever after, focus on the romance etc. Because the model is a box as below you can only map two factors at a time. So basically pick the two factors you're most interested in about your books and then it's time to map the current book market according to those two factors.

You then draw on the diagram names of books or publishers if they print similar books, according to the two factors you're mapping. For example, a book with a lot of sexual content would go on the far right side and if it was set around the world in luxury locations it would also go on the top of the box, so a Jackie Collins book would likely go top right hand corner of the box.

Repeat this for as many books you can think of until you've run out of books / publishers to map. Then look on the map and see where there's a gap in the map. This is literally, what marketeers call 'a gap in the market'.

Now, beware, there may be a gap in the market because those two factors together really don't make sense. It's up to you to make that call, but by systematically mapping out the positions of books in the market you are better placed to position your book in a less crowded area of the market – if that's what you want to do.

Alternatively, you may find there are lots of books in a certain area of the market, because that's the latest thing and then you decide to join that trend. Again, it's all about being strategic and thinking these things through. Doing this will help you describe your book to agents and publishers. When they ask is it like x author or y author you can say, it's less sexy than x but has a more international setting than y author. Then they will be able to see where your book fits in the market.

Glamour of location shown along the left side of the box, ranging from homely normal location bottom left corner to international jet set location top left corner.	
Sexual content from 0 bottom left to lots bottom right corner of the box.	

Here's a brand map for chocolate bars, something everyone can relate to!

Once you know where your book fits in the market, compared with others, you can then *position* yourself to the segment of customers to attract them to buy yours rather than competitors' books.

Using the example of chocolate bars, say you've developed a chocolate bar that's similar to Fererro Rocher – my favourite chocolate I could easily eat a whole box in one sitting – which is medium high quality and medium high price. By knowing that Fererro Rocher is similar to your new chocolate you can position yours as being more luxurious, of superior taste, or a more indulgent nature, than Fererro Rocher. You're pitching yourself as similar but better. Conversely, there would be no point in positioning your chocolate against a Twix because it would be much cheaper and of lower quality. It would be like comparing apples and oranges.

By looking at the wants and needs of each segment of customers you can position your book to ensure it meets their wants and needs better than any other books in a comparable position in the market. Comparing apples and apples, Fererro Rocher with a similar chocolate. You can then develop marketing communications (anything that communicates with your customers about your books) to show how your book best meets their wants and needs. And how do you do this? You create a *value proposition*. OK, yes, more marketing jargon and of course the marketing jargon klaxon so I'll explain what this means.

A *value proposition* must focus closely on what your customer wants and needs (from a product like yours) and how your product will make them think 'that's right for me, I'm buying it!'

How to create a value statement for your book in five steps

1) know your customer, what does she need, who is she, what problem is she wanting to solve, what does she value? If you don't know this you can research this online, or if you feel this is too US biased, you can do some desk research (Googling) of books similar to yours and find answers to these questions in their online review comments.

Taking a typical romance reader, which I've pulled together from the 2014 Romance Writers of America (RWA) survey about them:

- 84% of romance readers are women.
- Their average age is from 30 – 54 years old.
- In the United States, romance readers are most highly represented in the south, followed by the Midwest.
- Despite Janice Radway's 1984 study, *Reading the Romance,* about the Smithton women housewives in America who enjoyed romance, the demographic of female readers has changed along with the number of women in the workforce as a whole. 'Whether staying at home, working from home or working in an office, many women turn to romance novels for some entertainment, escape and relaxation at the end of the day.' (Rodale, 2015)
- More than half of the mass market paperbacks sold in the U.S. are romance
- Romance book buyers have an average income of $55,000.

What are they mostly reading? Well, according to the 2014 RWA survey:

Print: romantic suspense (53%); contemporary romance (41%); historical romance (34%); erotic romance (33%); New Adult (26%); paranormal romance (19%); Young Adult romance (18%); and Christian romance (17%).

E-book: romantic suspense (48%); contemporary romance (44%); erotic romance (42%); historical romance (33%); paranormal romance (30%); New Adult (26%); Young Adult romance (18%); and Christian romance (14%).

What tropes do they like to read?

Top ten popular romance tropes: (1) friends to lovers; (2) soul mate/fate; (3) second chance at love; (4) secret romance; (5) first love; (6) strong hero/heroine; (7) reunited lovers; (8) love triangle; (9) sexy billionaire/millionaire; (10) sassy heroine (ibid)

2) Now you know who your typical customer is and what she values, you need to work out how your book solves the problems your customer has. What value and results does your book offer your customers (that you know she'll value)?

How do you do this?

Research! But don't worry, it's only 'desk research' also known as a bit of judicious internet research.

And where do we find out what readers think about books similar to yours – in the same genre?

Amazon and Goodreads reviews…

So you've read reviews of books similar to yours and you've found out that your customers (or customers of books similar to yours) really love the period details of the 1950s when these books are set. You also find out that she likes this detail as it helps her remember what that time period was like when she was a young girl and that gives her an escape from her everyday life. And you find out that she loves to really root for a strong female heroine overcoming a series of challenges in her personal and love life.

So now you know what she values you need to describe how your book does all those things, how it includes all those elements and will give her a solution to wanting to remember the past, escape her present and live vicariously through a strong heroine.

3) Know your competitors/ comparators of similar books to your own. You should be well aware of this because you've just read their reviews online. Know which authors and books are competing for your customers' time and money in that sub genre of books. Now you need to explain how your book is better than your competitors – *Differentiate* in the DRIP model I've already explained. Why are your period descriptions better and more detailed than others? How is your heroine more life-like? How does she have to overcome more trials and tribulations with a smile on her face? How will your book provide a slice of nostalgic escape better than other similar books?

4) Now you pull all of this together in three to four short sentences in answer to the question: Why should I buy this book? Because the heroine is so real she'll feel like your friend and you'll want her to overcome the challenges the story throws at her. Because the period details are so perfect you'll step down memory lane and reminisce about the past, hence escaping your present effortlessly.

5) Now turn around the answer from step four into a statement and you have your very own value proposition. This could be for a specific book, or for you as an author and the types of books you write.

Publishers have also done it when their brand is above the author's name or book title. Mills and Boon has described its own books, on their covers, variously over the years as: 'Pure reading pleasure. Paperbacks that please. Romance for every mood. Makes any time special.' (Mills and Boon, various dates)

These straplines are also the value proposition to the customer. Based on what romance readers value from reading, they are guaranteeing to meet that need perfectly and every time.

New product development

In this context, this means publishing and writing new books. However, romance books do this in a specific way that means they are marking-led and therefore customer-led. And I'm going to explain how they do that in this section.

A lot of criticism is levelled at romance books because they're easy to read. Well, as someone with a communications background, the main purpose of writing is to communicate something to the reader. This is particularly important with the written word which is one way communication; unlike in a conversation, the reader can't ask the book or author what something means, while reading it. Communicating something to the reader requires clear, concise, simple words. This is not about the author showing off with long words and complex sentences that the reader finds herself marooned half way through and lost among the sentence. It is like that quote 'I didn't have time to write a short letter, so I wrote a long one instead' attributed to Mark Twain or Blaise Pascal depending on who you believe. (Quora, n.d.)

This basically says that it's much easier to blurt out lots of words that are unclear and rambling, than to craft a concise and easy-to-read shorter version. As someone who's taken complex technical descriptions from clinicians (nurses, doctors, physiotherapists) and senior managers and translated that – and I do mean *translated* because it was completely incomprehensible for the general public who were meant to be reading it – into plain English for patient and public leaflets and reports, I know and agree with that wholeheartedly. Why say 'operationalise the framework' when you can simply say 'do it' instead? Why indeed say, 'in the process of developing a bilateral conversation with key stakeholders' when you can say 'setting up a call with them' instead?

In 2013 Maya Angelou at the National Book Awards said, 'Easy reading is damn hard writing,' (Angelou, 2013 in Rodale, 2015). Anyone who's ever read literary fiction with pages and pages of introspection and long descriptions and beautiful metaphors and similes while simultaneously wondering 'what on earth is happening, who is this about, and where are we in the story?' will probably agree with me. I once read 60 pages of a beautifully written Booker Prize winning novel from the late nineties and honestly had absolutely no idea what was happening. Not. A. Clue.

I couldn't have told you any of the characters, what they were doing, what had happened, what they were thinking about. And I went to university, learned about existentialism, communications theory and postmodernism!

I'll analyse romance books' effortless writing style in Chapter 9 so you can bear this in mind when writing your next novel.

Romance, as a genre, uses something called semi-programmed issue to develop its new products / books. Semi-programmed issue is where books are 'distributed within a small circle [of regular readers] whose requirements are known and whose preferences have been thoroughly established.' (Escarpit, in Radway, 1991, p26) This means that romance publishers distribute their books to book stores, online retailers and then to readers, having fully understood their likes, needs, dislikes and wants from reading a romance book. This is why romance publishers have guidelines for the sort of stories they will and won't accept from authors. They know what their readers want and they only want to publish that sort of story. This isn't to say that all romance stories are the same, although there is a basic plot of a romance novel which I'll come onto later, however within this there are many different variations in setting, characters, conflicts, resolutions, all ultimately leading to a happy ending. (A similar argument can be made of crime fiction stories, and other genre fiction types, but any more of that's not for now.)

If you've ever written for a submission call that is also *semi-programmed issue*. The publisher is creating a set of rules for a series of stories that will be the same in key ways – setting, type of character, sort of conflict etc – while also being different. The readers will get similar pleasure from reading them and the stories will all tick certain boxes for readers who like that sort of book. It's semi-programmed issue because the authors write their own stories with their own characters, but within a strict set of parameters / framework that the publisher knows will please a certain number of readers based on previous sales.

Taking this idea a stage further, *fully-programmed issue* 'is characterized by the conscious creation of literary material for an already formally identified audience, usually through the mechanism of advance subscription' (Radway, 1991, p29). This method of developing new products (books) is both financially safe because the publisher knows roughly how many sales they will get of each category of romance through its subscription levels, but it also supports much more generic advertising approaches. Rather than having to develop a whole separate marketing campaign for each individual book, you simply advertise each 'line' and the benefits the reader will get from buying books in that line together. The trick to this sort of publishing is to provide the reader with the same type of pleasure again and again, but with different characters and conflicts. The setting is often not that different in fact the setting is very often the way these lines are categorised – historical, jet setting, medical, homely etc.

Examples of this subscription model include Mills and Boon / Harlequin book club where readers pick one or more lines and receives the books from that line every month. *The People's Friend*'s Weekly Pocket Novel subscription, Dreamspinner Press's Dream Spun Desires subscription model for various category romances by e-book or paperback are other models. In addition, there are various companies offering one book delivered per month that's picked based on the subscriber's reading preferences.

Both semi-programmed and fully-programmed issue are using the techniques in other areas of industry (fast moving consumer goods like soaps, tinned food etc) and applying it to book production. Before anyone starts throwing things at me, I am absolutely not criticising this.

Firstly, much popular fiction is actually purchased while people are doing their food shopping in the supermarket, so why shouldn't a book be thought of as a product just like a ready meal or some milk? Harlequin Mills and Boon revolutionised romance book selling by distributing their books in the places women most often went: chemists, supermarkets etc, rather than expecting them to go to book shops.

And secondly, one of the main reasons for writing this book is that romance, as a genre, is, I believe, one of the *most marketing-led genres of fiction.*

For this exact reason: if you trust a brand (of a publisher, author, or line of romance books) and enjoyed one book, then there's nothing wrong with picking another one.

As the teacher says, in Muriel Sparks' novel, *The Prime of Miss Jean Brodie*: "For those who like that sort of thing," said Miss Brodie in her best Edinburgh voice, "that is the sort of thing they like." (Sparks, 1961)

In other words, if you like floral patterned floaty dresses, why wouldn't you want to buy another one? If you enjoy comforting baked puddings, here's some more of those we also sell. And, just as Amazon includes the 'similar titles to what you've just bought' line underneath your current search, why wouldn't you welcome a publisher presenting you with more of the same but different type of books in a similar line?

Joseph McAleer puts it better than I could: 'The Mills & Boon imprint, like any successful commodity in a mass market, stands for a quality product, a kind of guarantee of an easy, thrilling, and satisfying read with an obligatory happy ending. This flavourful confection, wrapped in a brightly coloured paperback cover with a dreamy scene, is to many addictive in its escapist nature.' (McAleer in Vivanco, 2011, p14)

Please don't think I'm criticising this method of publishing. I am absolutely not. I've read a lot of romance books in these categories and enjoyed all of them to varying degrees. For me, as a typical romance reader, part of the pleasure of enjoying them is the comfort in the known; the comfort that I am absolutely sure that things will end well, but that along the way there will be new characters, new challenges and new conflicts to overcome. One of the appeals of romance with its emotion yet sure happy ending is contained jeopardy. Something we aren't guaranteed in real life.

After all, the fiction story isn't about the ending, but about the journey one goes on with the characters *to get to* the ending. Otherwise *Titanic* would be a very short film: The ship sinks.

I'll come on to why romance readers enjoy reading similar stories again and again; Radway covers this in detail in her study *Reading The Romance*. It's useful to understand this as a romance author, because then you can ensure you include those elements in your stories to make sure you give your customers moments of delight that will have them reaching for your next book again and again.

An important part of marketing, is new product development, as I've already covered, which in our context means writing new books. But to apply a marketing mindset to this (as the romance publishers do when buying new books, deciding on new 'lines' to develop or venturing into new niches within romance) you should do this having first done your research and planning, as already described. If you've researched what readers like (as Mills and Boon did many years ago, and still do today when deciding on new and declining lines) you're more likely to appeal to customers' tastes and therefore sell more books.

In addition, if you've done your wider marketing planning (looking at the PESTEL analysis of the wider environment and the book buying context) then you can make sure your new book will fit within that context well. Of course if you're a big name romance author you're more likely to just write what comes to you and your author brand name will carry you forward as many readers buy it on the basis of your name alone. However, for the other mere mortals among us, we can benefit from a bit more scientific and planned help. And it's also worth stating that even these big names will have some guidance and steering by their editor and publishers to help influence their next story to ensure it isn't completely at odds with the current trends and context of publishing and the way people live their lives.

Joanna Trollope's latest book, *City of Friends,* is about a group of high-powered business women working in the City of London. Maybe a bit late to the party of women in the workplace you could argue, but she has written about working women beforehand, it's just this is the first time she's focussed on the workplace and women's place in it. She conducted masses of research by interviewing women working in these jobs in the city while living there for a few months. I'm sure when she discussed this idea with her publisher and agent they would have given her guidance and suggestions on making this theme fresh and modern. Imagine if she'd decided to write a book set now about an unmarried woman in her twenties who became pregnant and was disowned by her family. It simply wouldn't reflect the lived experience of most women now, so it wouldn't sell.

Branding – this is another important part of what marketing does.

And what is a brand? *A brand is a promise to a customer about their product or service.* (Marsh, 2013)

As long as your books keep your promise to your customers – whatever that promise is – then you're golden. As soon as you start breaking your promise you're screwed.

I've already described the three main types of branding: author name, author visual branding and publishers so I won't go over it again.

The publisher branding comes back to my earlier point about semi-programmed and fully-programmed issue – by putting the publisher brand and its 'category' or 'line' more prominently than the book title or author name, that becomes the brand.

By buying a Mills and Boon Medical romance (from whoever, called whatever) the reader knows she's going to get 'Medical drama to set your pulse racing.' By enjoying a book (from whoever, called whatever) from their True Love line, she's going to enjoy 'Tender romances to touch the heart' and she's clear that any Historical book, from whichever author, about whatever subject will include 'Historical heroes to sweep you off your feet' (Mills and Boon, n.d.)

Before leaving branding I will end with two final thoughts. Sometimes an author's name branding can be so powerful that they continue to 'write' and publish books after their death. For example, Virginia Andrews who wrote eight books while she was alive but has subsequently 'written' approximately 80 after her death. Similarly, Harold Robbins has 'written' almost as many after his death as he did while he was alive, all selling very successfully. And this comes back to the point of a brand; if your author brand is your name and as long as all your books meet that brand promise readers will continue to buy regardless of who has actually written the books. It's a bit like buying a VW rather than a Seat, an Audi, or Skoda car when in fact they're all actually owned by the same parent company (VW Audi Group) and use the same underpinnings and are more often than not made in the same factory. Scandalous!

Things to remember

- STP – a framework to divide readers into groups with similar qualities (segmenting), making sure you target your marketing efforts to that group of people (targeting) and finally ensure your books are positioned – described, placed – in a way that is attractive to that group of readers.
- Value proposition – a step-by-step guide to developing a statement that describes why your book will meet the exact needs of your type of readers.
- New product development – writing new books by using a marketing mindset, including research etc.
- Fully-programmed issue – a subscription model of books being produced and sold to a pre-existing market of readers who want more similar books, using 'lines' or 'categories' of books, each with their own rules.

Things to consider

- Think about which segment of romance readers your books apply to and then consider how you can best reach them – where will they be hanging out online, in person for example?
- How do you feel about the concept of fully-programmed issue? Have you read stories from a romance category that can be bought in a subscription model? What are their similarities, what are their differences? Why would readers come back for more of the same?

Things to do

- Using customer feedback on similar books to your own, similar genre, similar setting etc, work through the value proposition steps and write a value proposition for your newest book. Why will your book fulfil the needs of readers who enjoy that sort of story?
- If you've never responded to a submission call, think about doing so. It will be a good experience of semi-programmed issue – or 'the same but different'. The publisher

will know there are readers wanting that sort of story, so it could be a way to get your name in front of a new group of readers.

• Go to a publisher's website that's putting out the kind of books you like and then to have a look at their submission guidelines just to see what their criteria are for putting out a book in that genre. This means you can understand what they're looking for – *the same*, and help you consider how to give yours a twist only you can do – *the different*.

CHAPTER 6 - What is a marketing strategy and how I can write one for myself as an author and for my books?

I'm often asked about a marketing strategy and what one is. I think some people think it's a mystical, magical thing that's very complicated. It's not.

I was once asked to develop a marketing strategy for a publisher as a marketing consultant. So why should you, an author, care about a marketing strategy when you've got a publisher to do all that for you?

Well, in my experience, unless you're a big brand name author or with a big publisher, authors are expected to do most of their own promotion. After the actual publishing of the book, maybe sending out some advance reader copies (ARCs) for reviews, and perhaps if you're lucky, getting your book in the distribution channels (the *Place*, or where it's sold, which apart from online is a valuable role of a publisher as an author is unlikely to get their book in a chain of bookshops or supermarkets) there may not be much actual marketing done by the publisher.

At its most basic level, a marketing strategy is the *what* you're going to do in terms of marketing.

Now, you're probably thinking what more does this need to be than simply 'sell lots of books'? Well, there are a few different marketing strategies you can consider. And depending on which one you pick, that will affect the rest of the marketing strategy. Don't worry, I'm going to talk through this step-by-step in a way that will support you to do the same.

If you're published by a big publisher there's no reason you can't take some ideas about this to them to hand when they're developing your own marketing strategy with their marketing department. Having an author who's marketing savvy will be a wonderful change for them, I'm sure.

In addition, if you're indie publishing, or published by a smaller publisher that's basically not doing much marketing, then they're *your* books, so you should take charge and decide on *your* own marketing strategy. As I said at the start of the book, marketing isn't something done by 'those people' in a distant place 'over there,' so as an author you should take responsibility for making these decisions yourself. After all, the most important aspect of the marketing mix, Product, is all from you. They're your books, so why wouldn't you want to take control of where and how they're sold?

Taking a systematic approach to a marketing strategy as I will describe below, means you're focussing your efforts in a *planned strategic* way rather than in a scattergun knee-jerk way. Remember the example of needing more space at home in the first chapter? You don't want to spend lots of time placing some adverts, or changing your pricing or maybe trying to get some PR placed if you're not clear what your overall aim is.

Now I'll go through the main sections you'd need in a marketing strategy:

Introduction – you don't necessarily need this, but you can think of it as a summary to introduce what the strategy is going to cover, what its main purpose is and who's authored it. Probably a good idea to write this once you've finished writing the whole strategy.

An audit / research – this is where you include the results of an audit. An audit is where you look at your current sales, which books sell best, through which outlets, at which times of year. You can include results of any previous marketing efforts you've done – placing adverts, selling at conferences etc. I'd suggest going back twelve months as a minimum and it could include multiple years of data that you've analysed. The important thing here is to be looking at trends, and trying to draw conclusions from the data. It's no good including data for the sake of data here. The analysis and internal audit you go through should all link back to what your objectives are. No 'it would be nice to look at' because that will just muddy the water. You want to keep focussed on outcomes (improvements).

You should also include some information about the time taken and costs of various marketing efforts. So for example if you've attended three book fairs, how much did that cost, what was the return on investment in terms of sales. Remember, you are a business. Imagine you're having to account for costs to a finance director and justify spend for next year. I know that effectively you are the finance director, the HR director and the chief executive, but it's still important to take stock, go through this process to evaluate what worked and what didn't work.

In addition to internal data, here is where you'd also include results from a wider PESTEL analysis in relation to your main objectives. Just a few sentences for each factor that shows you've thought through each of the six elements and how that affects books, publishing, and therefore you.

You should also include the results of any research you've conducted to inform this strategy. And remember, *marketing decisions should always be informed by sound research.* It doesn't need to be finding new data by asking questions – it could easily be pulling together existing data to inform decisions you want to make in the strategy. For example if you're thinking of withdrawing your paperbacks from self-publishing, you should look at data on sales of romance books based on format to see if that would buck or go with the trend. There are links to sources of this data in the Bibliography.

If you're thinking of increasing your sales of your books to America it would be good to look at the top selling books in your sub genre of romance and looking at customer reviews about what they like and dislike – is this something you can use in your next book idea?

If you have a group of heavy user customers who buy everything you publish, you could ask them a series of questions about what they would value in terms of value added to your books – free samples of next books, meeting you to get their books signed, being involved in beta reading stories etc.

SMART corporate and marketing objectives

As we're thinking about your writing career as a small business you need some SMART corporate / business objectives, and then you write some SMART marketing objectives to support those.

SMART = Specific, Measurable, Achievable, Realistic, Timed.

For example, say you want to make more money as an author. That's not specific, measurable, achievable realistic or timed, so let's break it down.

You have a business objective A) of increasing author income by 15% during the next tax period and you have another business objective, B) to reduce your author costs by 10% over the same period. Those are SMART (they may not be realistic depending on your current levels of income and costs, but let's go with it, OK?)

There's no point in saying you'll increase your author income while also increasing your author costs because that will not result in an overall increase in the amount of money you make. However, if your overall objective was to spread your author brand around the world you may want to increase income as well as increase costs by attending conferences around the world. It all depends on what your overall business objective is.

So taking those two business objectives you now break them down into marketing objectives that relate to aspects of the marketing mix (the 7 Ps).

Business objective A) To increase author income by 15% over the next tax year period

Marketing objectives – to support the delivery of the business objective A)
To increase sales in the UK by 5% over the next tax year period through sales this will be achieved through:
1. Product – to write two more books than in the previous tax year using themes / topics of other popular books in the genre
2. Price – to reduce the price of the first book in a series, to reduce the price when a new book is launched for two weeks
3. Promotion – to promote your books in targeted places online to reach more of the same segment of customers (online magazines, blogs)
4. Place – to widen the outlets where your books are available from only Amazon to include iBooks, Kobo etc… To liaise with local book shops about getting paperbacks in there. To appear at two book sales / conferences to sell books in person.

Business objective B) To decrease author costs by 10% over the next tax year period

Marketing objectives – to support the delivery or business objective B
1. Product – to reduce editing and cover art costs by X%
2. Price – this is the only part of the marketing mix that makes money so it's not appropriate to discuss it here. I'm including it to explain why you wouldn't include it.

3. Promotion – to reduce costs on flyers / bookmarks by Y% and cut out the appearance at conferences where there is no opportunity to sell books.

4. Place – to sell self published books on your own website hence cutting out income to third party vendors by z date.

Ansoff matrix

There are four different marketing strategies and this matrix lays them out for you to see.

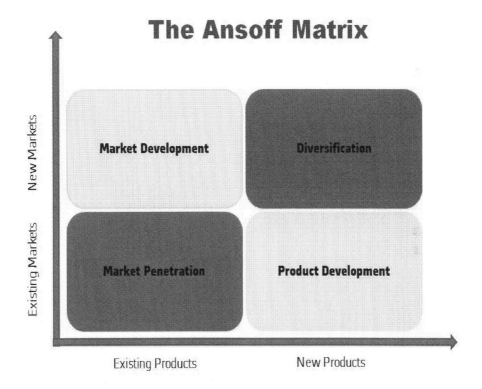

(image from Wikipedia, JaisonAbeySabu)

The easiest option is to sell more of the same books to your existing customers, Market Penetration in the model. This is easiest because you already have a relationship with these customers, they like the products you already sell them. This may require writing more books per year than you'd previously managed. It may mean encouraging your existing customers to buy two or three different books (or the same as a gift) when previously they'd only buy one at a time.

The next easiest option is to sell the same books to a new set of customers – in a different country, in a different customer segment, however you want to focus this. This is Market Development in the model. This is where you sell your current type of books, your back catalogue, the new books you write in the genre you're already known for, to a new group of customers. This could mean translating the books and selling in non-English speaking countries. It could mean selling to a different age group from your current customers' age profile. It could mean selling to more men when most of your customers are women. When thinking through which segment of customers you want to sell to, it's important to have done your STP first. Which is the most profitable segment? Which segment is the easiest to reach? Once you know this, you can then think through marketing approaches to reach that segment.

Then we come to selling new products to your existing customers – Product Development in the model. This isn't more of the same books, this is a different type of product to your existing customers. Say you write historical romances this would mean selling contemporary romances to your loyal existing customers. Or you could sell crime fiction to your romance readers. Or, it could mean selling manuscript appraisals or places on writing workshops or another writing related product / service to your existing customers.

Changing the type of product you produce is called Diversification in the model. You know how Easyjet used to sell flights, and then they started selling holidays, and then insurance, and then car hire? Diversification. Here you're using your name as the brand (as Easyjet did) for the other services and products.

This is really quite hard because you're changing track, venturing into the unknown because not all of your existing customers will want your new products. It's usual to diversify in a related area (books, publishing etc) rather than a whole different business area.

Look at what Easyjet did, those services are all related to travel / holidays etc. If an author suddenly started trying to sell cookery classes it would be unlikely to work well because that's not an expectation of the author's brand. Another good example is where Tesco tried to sell in a network of small shops in America. Americans hadn't heard of Tesco. Tesco isn't renowned for its small shops, it's better known for large and medium sized stores stocking a wider variety of products including homeware and electricals. Tesco shortly abandoned this venture at a loss.

So that's the Ansoff Matrix – it's a model to think strategically about how you're going to expand your business of selling your products to readers.

Let's turn back to the marketing strategy headings.

Customers – this is where, in your marketing strategy, you'd include a brief summary of your customers. Where they buy from, which places they buy most from, what their demographic profile is, what their likes and dislikes are (from reviews or talking to them face to face). The more you understand and know your customers, the better you'll be at positioning (framing, phrasing, expressing – more detail in the STP section we've covered) your marketing communications (anything that communicates to your customers – flyers, blogs, articles, videos etc) to them in a way that's most appealing / engaging for them and most likely to result in sales.

Your products – describe the range of books / services if you do workshops etc that you currently sell. Explain which sub genre of romance they fit into, add in some similar comparator books within the same sub genre.

List how many and what type of books you have currently published, how long until you receive the rights back, how many and what type of books you have in draft. This is about encapsulating your current 'stock' of books at various stages. It's important to capture it all here, because depending on your marketing strategy, according to the Ansoff Matrix, you may need to quickly bring out a lot of new books in a short time. It's also worth covering here which are your best selling books – of all time, in their first six months, which are seasonal favourites (Christmas books for example). It's about taking a look back at all of your books / services and looking at which ones bring you in the most money. If you're self published, you should include the cost to publish each book and the estimated time until it breaks into profit at current sales. Rest assured companies that manufacture products do this as part of their product life cycle. A car often doesn't go into profit until year two or three of production.

Communications – how do you currently communicate with your customers about your books? Looking at the full range of marketing communications, are there any gaps with types of communications you're currently using? Do you not use adverts or flyers at the moment. Have you tried PR but it's not worked well. Do you only use social media in one way and not also to communicate to your readers about your books?

The most appropriate marketing mix (Product, Price, Place, Promotion etc) to deliver your marketing strategy. This is where you would go into more detail about the marketing mix to best meet your marketing objectives. Here you go through each of the four (or seven) Ps and explain what you're going to do to meet the marketing objectives. I'll take a few from the marketing objectives above to illustrate:

- Product – in addition to already planned new books, to write one x 65,000 word book similar to x popular book including the themes of family, work and vampires. Ensure the title includes the words 'y' as per other popular books in the sub genre. Write three x 25,000 word linked novellas with B heroine from D series (that is selling well, or links well with the current trends and themes in books or wider society).

- Price – (only possible to have complete control with your self published titles, although you could suggest ideas re pricing to your publisher) have first book in Z series free for four months. Make Xmas novella 99p for all of November. All new books to start at 99p for two weeks, and then back up to normal length-based price.

- Promotion – To promote your books in A, B, C and D Facebook groups on topics about horses, the East End of London and jet setting holiday locations. Place four opinion pieces / interviews about current books and new books with E, F, G, H review websites / blogs / online e-magazines. Approach I, J, K L women's magazines for short story places. Approach Y, Z local radio stations and local papers with stories about how my cat saved me from a burning building and how I wrote about that in Z new book…Remember a PR piece has to be a story not just 'I have a new book out'.

- Place – to widen the outlets where your books are available from only Amazon to include iBooks, Kobo etc… To liaise with local book shops about getting paperbacks in there. To appear at two book sales / conferences to sell books in person.

How to measure success – The final section of a marketing strategy is success measures. How are you going to measure if your marketing strategy works?

It may not only be sales. If your business objective was to increase your visibility in America it could be the number of readers you interact with while at conferences in America and the number of social media followers / friends from America.

If your flyers / book marks have a promotion code on them for customers to use when they contact you for their free book (or whatever you're offering) then you can track where that customer interaction has come from, rather than it just being random luck.

Remember those SMART marketing objectives? This is where you look back at them to check whether you've achieved what you've said you're going to measure.

It's also worth not leaving this until the end of the year to review. If you're in the middle of doing something and you're not seeing any result, make sure you've given it time, and then change your strategy. No point flogging a dead marketing strategy.

So that's what you'd include in a marketing strategy, and we've reached the end of this chapter.

Things to remember

- **Marketing strategy** – this is a document that outlines what you're going to do to market your books. It has a series of headings which you should use to think systematically and strategically about how you're going to market your books.

- **Ansoff matrix** – is a four box diagram describing four different strategies you could use to market your products, including – new products and new markets. It's a framework to focus your thinking on which of the four approaches you'll use, rather than trying to do all four at the same time and failing.

Things to consider

- When you've been trying to sell more books have you considered which of the four strategies you're going to do as described in the Ansoff Matrix?

- Have you ever thought about what your marketing objectives are, as an author? I mean, any more specifically than 'sell more books'?

- Have you ever looked at your sales by book, by country, by place (Amazon, Kobo, book shops etc)?

Things to do

- This is going to be hard, because now we're deep into marketing speak and you'll probably just turn the page and move onto the next chapter. You may feel like you're sinking in a quagmire of marketing jargon. Don't panic! As I've shown, most of the marketing speak is just terms for things you already know, or they're frameworks to structure thinking. Now I'd like you to have a go at writing your own marketing strategy. Work through the headings in this chapter and think about each section. You'll know better than anyone else the answers to most of the questions posed by each section. Why? Because they're your books. Because it's your career as an author.

- If writing a whole marketing strategy seems too hard, just look at the Ansoff Matrix and think about which of the four options you'd like to focus on in the next twelve months.

- Now write a few SMART marketing objectives to support that. Yes, I mean you! Go on!

- Now have a large glass of wine, and congratulate yourself on reaching half-way through this book!

CHAPTER 7 - What is a marketing plan and how I can write one for myself as an author and my books?

We've covered the marketing strategy which is the *what*, and now we move onto the marketing plan which is basically the *how*. Have you heard of the phrase, 'fail to plan, plan to fail'? Well this is where you need to think through exactly *how* you're going to achieve all the wonderful things you've said you're going to do in the marketing strategy.

This may well be the point at which you realise that since most of these things will probably come down to you to do, you've given yourself too much to do. And that's fine. So go back to the marketing strategy and ask yourself:

- Is this really important for me to meet my business objective and therefore my marketing objective?
- Can I pay someone else to do this for me?
- Can I do this in quarter two or three or four of the year rather than trying to do it all in quarter one?

The marketing plan doesn't need to be fancy or with lots of narrative and explanation, you should have already covered that in your marketing strategy.

The marketing plan can simply be a table:

What you're doing	Who's doing it	How you'll do it	When	Progress
Lift these from the marketing objectives numbered before. Make sure it's broken down into clear specific separate tasks to complete. You can go into as much detail as you like or keep things broad. I'd keep it somewhere in the middle so it's clear and actionable but not too detailed.	Divide this up into the different parts of the *what* – the thing – that is being done.	Think about whether you need information to do the tasks in the first column. Do you need to research that, buy it, ask someone?	I'd suggest staggering this across each of the four quarters of the year rather than trying to do it all at once.	This marketing plan should be a living document you update as you do things. Quite apart from keeping you on track it's a good motivator to see you're moving forwards towards your marketing goals.

Things to remember
- An idea (a strategy) without how to do it (a plan) is basically a wish.
- Think through how you're going to make all the things you've said you'll do in your marketing plan actually happen. Write it down, step by step.
- Now go back and ask yourself the questions in this chapter.

Things to consider
- Have you ever considered which parts of marketing you can ask others to do for you?
- Have you ever thought about reviewing your progress against what you've said you'll do throughout the year?

Things to do
- Go back to the marketing strategy you wrote. If you didn't write it before, now please give it a go. It doesn't need to be pages and pages, just a few bullet points under each section. Now add a table at the end of the marketing strategy and write down how you're going to make those things happen, step by step, and who's going to do it.
- Remember, you don't need to do it all yourself.
- Reward yourself with a rather large glass of your favourite drink, and then read a few chapters of a blissfully escapist romance book!

CHAPTER 8 - Romance as a genre – data

And now to turn to romance as a genre. The reason I felt a book about marketing for romance authors needed to be written is because romance, as a genre, is commercially successful – one of, if not the biggest segments of fiction book sales – it attracts voracious readers, and some of the most popular tropes and sub-genres are all very popular in the romance genre.

And why do we want to know this data?

So we can knowingly use this data to inform our writing in future: the what we write, the how we write it, the how it's published and the how much we write too.

Romance and erotica sales were over $1400 million, compared with crime / mystery at $700 million, religious / inspirational at another $700 million, science at just under $600 million and finally horror at under $100 million. (Dalke, 2016)

In America, 89% of romance sales are digital (ebooks). Of those, 57% are self-published, 21% are from the big five publishers and 10% are from small or medium publishers. As authors, this means that the opportunities for indie publishing are enormous, and that if self-publishing a paperback sounds like too much to get your head around, the majority of readers won't mind because they're used to buying in digital format already. (ibid)

Looking at the P for Place now...In America, 74% of all romance digital book sales are through Amazon.com. This means that if you're wanting to self-publish, you could stick to just Amazon format and reach nearly ¾ of your e-book audience. It makes it less time consuming to create the different e-book formats and upload to other vendors. (Guy, 2016)

Turning to the P for Product now...Research shows that the sub genres of romance that earn the most money are: contemporary, romantic comedy, new adult and mystery and suspense.

Thinking about the Price now...the price points that earn the most money are $3.99 and $2.99, then $4.99, with $0.99 earning the fourth largest amount of money. $1.99 is a dead zone in terms of amount earned. This is likely because it's twice as much as the cheapest price point at which readers think they'll give a book a try because it's so cheap, but it's not moving into the $3.99 price point where quality is perceived as being higher. Readers attach a value to something based on its price. Something really can be too cheap and therefore will be associated in buyers' minds as being of inferior quality. This is probably where the $1.99 price point falls down. (ibid)

Long-term earnings vary wildly between different types of publishers. Big five publisher titles' earnings drop off very quickly, with sales plummeting to low levels after one to two months. This is likely related to the way they're promoted (cheap prices at the start with buy one get one half price, or two books for a reduced price) and the place where they're for sale (supermarkets, high street book shops in prominent places, airports). But once their moment in the limelight has passed, the big five publisher is onto the next thing. This is why, there tends to be only a few big phenomenon books each year. The sales numbers for the top one or two of each of these books that are promoted heavily and in places where readers are likely to see them forces a few big name books into everyone's consciousness. The year of *50 Shades of Grey* I talked to a baggage handler at a UK airport and he said that *literally* every woman's hand luggage had a copy of that book in it during that summer. And then, everyone had moved onto the next big book. (ibid)

Conversely, indie published books continue earning and selling in respectable numbers sometimes even three plus years after their release. In this case, there are no supermarket shelves or book shop piles to come down from. There's also no heavy discounting promotions to pull back from, resulting in lower sales. Chances are an indie author will put the book available online in one or two web places, and leave them there all the time.

How many titles does an author need published before their name 'breaks out there'? Well, research shows that more titles does mean more income, but per title earnings only double between an author's first published title and their twentieth title. So in summary, it's a long slog, but eventually you may get there. (ibid)

Things to remember
- Although much maligned, romance, as a genre is keeping the book industry profitable.
- Being aware of up-to-date industry data doesn't mean you have to follow the trends, or even use the information, but at least if you're ignoring it, you're doing so knowingly.
- You may not be the next big book, but as an indie published author, your sales will be likely to tail off much slower than the big name books.

Things to consider
- Did you know how romance fits among the other fiction genres in terms of sales?
- Why do you think romance readers are most likely to read e-books than paperbacks?
- Why is the demographic of romance readers massively skewed towards women?
- Is there anything you could do to attract more male readers?

Things to do

• See if you can find any more research and data about the romance genre. Romance authors' organisations (The Romantic Novelists' Association, Romance Writers of America, Romance Writers of Australia) often publish annual reports on the state of the industry so it's worth looking out for them.

• Look in a supermarket at how many books for sale are romance – as in have romance as a part of the plot, even if they're not a category romance – compared to the other genres of books.

• Search on Amazon.com and Amazon.co.uk for genres and see how many titles are listed under romance. Compare this to crime, non-fiction, and other categories.

CHAPTER 9 - Romance as a genre – making sure your books match up to readers' genre expectations

I've already explained the marketing mix (the 4 Ps or the 7 Ps) but the most important part of that, without which you have nothing to promote, sell, place or anything to give physical evidence about, is PRODUCT.

So to really understand what a romance book is, I'd like to turn to a clear definition from Daphne Clair and Robyn Donald, prolific Harlequin Mills and Boon authors: romances tell 'a story in which the plot is driven by a sexually based emotional relationship between two people. And for most readers there has to be a happy ending – or at least the strong implication of future happiness'. (in Vivanco, 2011, p12)

I like that definition because it's not specific about the gender of the two people, because especially in recent years, the popularity of male male romance among mainly female readers and authors, has taken off out of slash fan fiction. There is also a growing lesfic genre of women-loving-women stories. And in a world where same sex marriage exists – in some countries – specifying that a romance needs to involve a man and a woman feels pretty out-of-date. Obviously, with shifter romance, the relationship could be between two tree shifters, or wolf shifters of various genders, depending on the genre of the story, but the main take away is that it's about two beings with human emotions and characteristics.

Penny Jordan, who wrote romances over 30 years sums up the main concept of a romance novel well, 'At the end of the day everything I write is about relationships.' (in Flood, 2010)

I think the happy ending aspect is important for a large majority, if not all readers of particularly category romances, and I agree with the RWA definition: 'a central love story and an emotionally satisfying and optimistic ending'. (in Vivanco, 2011, p12) In her 1984 study, Janice Radway finds the Smithson women she interviewed describe the two most important ingredients of a romance novel are 'a happy ending' and 'a slowly but consistently developing love between hero and heroine'. (in Regis, 2013, p22)

Taking a more scientific approach to this, Radway analyses the plot of the romance novels her focus group of readers identified as their favourites. Radway agrees with Will Wright's critique of Propp (who boiled down stories into a set of functions), 'that a genre is never defined solely by its constitutive set of functions, but by interaction between characters and their development as individuals.' (Radway, 1991, p120) In other words, the genre of romance isn't defined by having a set series of things that happen in the plot, but by the way the characters behave together and develop from the start to the end of the story.

Having read a lot of critiques and analysis about this, and having read *an awful lot* of category romance and broader popular romantic fiction novels, I think, like most things, it's a bit of both.

To truly write a five out of five star romance novel in the eyes of the readers (because after all it's about the customers' perception and screw what the critics think because basically romance is dead in the water as far as their snobby views are concerned), you need *both* to ensure the characters develop and interact together in certain ways, *and* to cover a series of specific functions in the plot. Pamela Regis, in *A Natural History of the Romance Novel* helpfully outlines the eight functions of the romance plot, which I'll come onto very shortly.

Before I do – and I'm sure some of you are either rubbing your hands in glee thinking it'll be an easy step by step guide to writing your next and every future romance book afterwards, that this is finally the oft-spoken about 'formula' for the romance novel – it isn't. I'll just pause for a few other points.

The basic romance plot, although clearly dividing the story up into eight chunks, doesn't tell you anything about the who, what, where, why, when and how. It simply tells you a broad list of romance plot elements that should happen in the story. It also doesn't prescribe an order in which these elements happen either. This means, naturally that the details of those eight elements are completely up to the author's imagination.

There are only eight main notes of music, but there are multi millions of different combinations making different songs. Same with these eight elements. It's in the who, what, where, why, when and how that makes each romance book different.

And, according to Brooker, while researching *The Seven Basic Plots*, he identifies a pattern underlying stories in five stages: 'from the initial mood of anticipation, through a "dream stage" where all seems to be going unbelievably well, to the "frustration stage" when things begin to go mysteriously wrong, to the "nightmare stage" where everything goes horrendously wrong, ending in that final moment of death and destruction.' (Brooker, 2004, p4)

And so he found a pattern in stories about self-destruction with an unhappy ending, he analysed stories with a happy ending and eventually wrote *The Seven Basic Plots* which explains that overall, he concludes there are only seven basic plots in existence. He caveats this by saying that there 'are extensive areas of overlap between one type of plot and another. Indeed, there are many stories which are shaped by more than one "basic plot" at a time…There are still other stories which are shaped by only part of such a plot.' (Brooker, 2004, p6) It all comes down to how far back you're going to stand when analysing a story.

You could break down a story to three simple stages: equilibrium, disequilibrium, new equilibrium. Because, after all, a story isn't a story if something doesn't happen.

An aside about an editor friend. She once received a submission and right in the middle of the book, she found this: ***SOMETHING HAPPENS*** This speaks straight to the point that in a story something must change, something must happen, otherwise it's not a story, or if it is, it's a very dull one.

Have you ever read a book or watched a film that leaves you dissatisfied and wondering what that was all about and why indeed you wasted your time on it? I know I have. Brooker asserts that these stories are 'failing fully to realise the basic plot which lies behind it.' (ibid) So now we know the context that, depending on how you look at it, there could be one story in the world based on the disturbance and return of equilibrium, or there could be seven basic plots, listed below with a romance slant added by me:

1. Overcoming the monster – escaping a relationship or the emotional scars of the past to find a lover.

2. Rags to riches – the contrast of settings provides an opportunity for love.

3. The quest – to find a lover, to find who the main character is and love themselves and then find a lover.

4. Voyage and return – in search for a lover, for someone who really 'gets' the main character deeply. It could be searching for love but finding it was there all along – like looking for love but realizing you've been in love with your best friend the whole time.

5. Comedy – the trials and tribulations of dating.

6. Tragedy – err, maybe not...but perhaps a romance that ends sadly in the death of one character. Is that truly a romance then...discuss?

7. Rebirth – after leaving a previous relationship, finding a new lover who brings the character out of her shell to rebirth into a new woman. (Brooker, 2004)

From this if you imagine a few of your favourite romance stories I'm sure you can conclude that romances could fit within at least six of these broad plots.

Penny Jordan, the acknowledged queen of Mills and Boon with 187 under her hard-working belt before she sadly passed away in 2012, says in a *Guardian* interview, 'It is very difficult to have a new take on an old story, and romance is an old story – it's been there forever. It has to ring true to the reader but at the same time you have to write in a way that keeps them turning pages,' And it's that new way, fresh look, new conflicts, that make romance novels an endless variation on an old story. (in Flood, 2010)

So, with all of this in mind I'm now, finally, going to cover Regis' eight elements of the basic romance plot.

The definition of society that the romance novel will reform

This is basically the setting in which the main characters find themselves.

It is the physical setting (a hospital, an airport, an office etc) as well as the setting in terms of time period.

But the important element here is that, 'This society is in some way flawed; it may be incomplete, superannuated, or corrupt. It always oppresses the heroine and hero.' (Regis, 2013, p31) Why does it oppress them? Because we need conflict. This is the external conflict that drives the story forward, that keeps the two, hero and heroine (or two heroes, or two heroines) apart.

The amount of detail included in the society varies depending on the type of romance. A longer women's popular fiction novel of say 90,000 words up to 200,000 in some instances, written by authors such as Penny Vincenzi, Jackie Collins, Jilly Cooper among others, has a lot more wordage to include the detail of this society and the conflicts. However, a category romance, which tend to be about 50,000 words, maybe up to 75,000 for historical ones, has the society 'barely sketched – the heroine and hero may be the only representatives of it that we see...In historical romance novels the society is carefully drawn and its unfamiliar principles explained.' (ibid) The reason for this is that historical readers are reading that type of romance specifically *for* the details, *for* the differences between that setting and the time in which they live now, to be explained. Unlike a contemporary category romance where a farmhouse, a bedroom, a farm yard, are simply explained as only that, and the reader is left to fill in the blanks herself. With only 50,000 words in an average length category romance, the author doesn't have much space to have long meandering descriptions of everyday objects when simply 'the farmhouse' will do, and the reader would much prefer to read about the character's feelings, emotions, internal anguish than descriptive details like the *blue dilapidated Ford* tractor was parked against the *grey thatched stone* farmhouse and the expansive yard was muddy with a spattering of leaves on the ground. And so the descriptions could go on...

The meeting between hero and heroine
'Usually near the beginning of the novel, but also sometimes presented in flashback, the heroine and hero meet for the first time. Some hint of the conflict to come is often introduced.' (Regis, 2013, p31)

With readers' attention spans shortening since the advent of the internet and being time-poor, many genre romances often start with the hero and heroine (or hero and hero, or heroine and heroine) meeting or clashing within the first few pages. Although it sounds cliché, and the reader knows he and she will end up together, it's about the how, and the when, and the why, and the what emotional and external conflicts they must overcome to reach the happy ending, that keeps the romance readers turning the pages. I've included some openings of romance novels to illustrate this later in the book.

An account of their attraction for each other

'A scene or scenes scattered throughout the novel establishes for the reader the reason that this couple must marry.' (Regis, 2013, p33) As well as marry in the modern world, it can also mean simply be together. The key element here is that it mustn't happen too early, or be too easy to fulfill. Otherwise they meet on page one, confess their undying love for one another and they're together by page four and the book's over by page six. No.

'The attraction keeps the heroine and hero involved long enough to surmount the barrier.' (ibid) Attraction must be more than simply physical, it 'can be based on a combination of sexual chemistry, friendship, shared goals or feelings, society's expectations, and economic issues.' (ibid) In other words, these things combine to be described as love. Not to assume anything, even within the romance genre, Regis also adds that some 'romance novels interrogate this notion of love, others simply assume it.' (ibid)

So there's plenty of latitude on what love comprises, whether or not it is love, and whether the elements described do genuinely add up to something the characters experience as love. Sounds pretty complex to me, especially for a genre described as formulaic, don't you think?

The barrier between them

'A series of scenes often scattered throughout the novel establishing for the reader the reasons that this heroine and hero cannot marry.' (Regis, 2013, p32) Note this isn't one scene, it's a series of scenes. If it were only one scene, again, it would be a very short, boring and emotionally dissatisfying romance book. Because a romance novel is focussed on the developing relationship, it therefore follows that the 'romance novel's conflict often consists entirely of this barrier between the heroine and hero.' (ibid) In other words, don't throw in other conflicts not related to the romance; readers aren't interested and it'll slow down and mess up the main plot. The barrier that exists between them is also more commonly described by editors, publishers, authors, as conflict. These barriers, or conflicts, 'can be external, a circumstance that exists outside of a heroine or a hero's mind,' otherwise known as external conflict or plot, such as the place or time in which the story is set, as well as 'internal, a circumstance that comes from within either [the hero and heroine] or both.' (Regis, 2013, p32) The internal or emotional conflict can be further divided into personal conflict related to one character – how her own emotional issues hold her back from a happy ending. And another internal conflict, romantic conflict. This is why the two main characters can't and don't get along together; it's how their own personal internal conflicts interact with each other to form an impossible barrier to their being together. A man who can't open up to a woman since he blames the death of his ex-girlfriend on himself. A woman who can't be with a man who has a daughter because the woman doesn't want to be a mother.

The declaration of heroine and hero that they love each other

'The scene or scenes in which the hero declares his love for the heroine, and the heroine her love for the hero, can occur anywhere in the narrative.' (Regis, 2013, p34) So it's important that it happens, because, after all it's a romance, but it doesn't need to happen in any particular point during the story. Placing this declaration at different points, 'helps create a variety of plots within the set of possibilities open to the romance novel.' (ibid) By having this declaration of love near the start of the novel when they first meet means 'the novel presents a love-at-first-sight situation.' (ibid) This provides all sorts of opportunities for comedy because the heroine doesn't need to be persuaded of her love for the hero, but instead the hero needs to be freed from things that prevent her from marrying him – parents, work, a current partner etc. Alternatively, by moving this declaration scene to the end of the story, 'and the heroine and hero declare their love for each other after the novel's barrier has been surmounted; often enough, the barrier was their inability or unwillingness to declare for each other, and the declaration scene marks the end of this barrier.' (ibid) So even though the hero and heroine love one another, they're unable to express it verbally to one another due to internal and external conflicts, until right at the end, after which they've worked through their issues to be together. In addition, the declaration scene for hero and heroine can be separate, such as in *Pride and Prejudice* where 'Darcy declares for Elizabeth in the middle of the novel...[and] Elizabeth declares for Darcy at the end of the novel' meaning that it's 'presenting instead the slow development of love and regard between heroine and hero.' (Regis, 2013, p35) In summary – there's almost endless variety in how this element can be covered too.

The point of ritual death

This is often called the 'oh sh*t' or 'the black' moment in popular fiction. It's the point when you're sure all is lost, the hero won't save the day, the heroine will never see the hero again and it's all turning to hell in a handcart.

In a romance novel it's 'the moment in the narrative when the union between heroine and hero, the hoped-for resolution, seems absolutely impossible, when it seems that the barrier will remain, more substantial than ever.' (Regis, 2013, p35)

This is a key moment in a genre that places so much importance on a happy ending. At this point, the 'happy ending is most in jeopardy.' (ibid) The reason for this, even though an experienced romance reader knows *all will definitely end well*, is the emotional response this point creates in the reader as she 'responds to the peril, the mood, and to the repetition of the imagery of death.' (ibid) Here, I take death as being of the relationship, since rarely does anyone die in a romance novel, and a hero and heroine would not die, since their happy ever after would hence be precluded. Romance novels are so popular because they provide *contained jeopardy* through this element of the story, followed by a guaranteed happy ending.

I've included a few examples to illustrate how this can be shown in romances, using less than 400 words:

Back in Her Husband's Arms by Susanne Hampton

'The plane leaves in just over four hours so I must go-'

'Have a good flight.' Tom's husky voice cut in.

Sara spun round to find him standing very close to her. She wanted to reach out and hold him, to touch his face and feel his arms around her. But he kept a distance between them and she did the same.

'I went home and found you'd left so I thought I'd come and tidy up.' He took a step back as she turned and she knew better than to close the even bigger space he had created.

With tears moistening her cheeks, she looked across at the man she loved. Marjorie left them alone and busied herself in her office, closing the door behind her to give them privacy to say goodbye.

'I hope I've left everything in order.'

'I'm sure you have.' He said nothing about the tears, which he couldn't have missed.

'Take care, Tom.'

'You too, Sara, and if you need anything just call.' Tom wanted to hold her but he knew that it would break him. He would make a promise he couldn't keep, just so she would stay a little while longer. That would be selfish. 'I'll stay in touch and when the time comes I will provide you with whatever you need or want. I promise you.'

'I'll be fine,' she reassured him. But she wouldn't turn to face him. She didn't want to look deep into his deep grey eyes. It was over. Finally over. He clearly had no problem with her leaving.

She had no idea what she would be doing in a month. Except trying to start a life somewhere without him.

'Sara, you will never want for anything.'

Except for a husband and a father, she thought as she walked away.

Squaring her shoulders the way she had when she'd first arrived, Sara made her way to the door. She knew Tom was watching her. She willed him to chase after her and ask her to stay.

He didn't.

He let her go. (Hampton, 2014, pp175-176)

Falling For The Bridesmaid by **Sophie Pembroke**

'You know the worst part?' Violet asked. 'I actually trusted you. All that talk about never trusting anyone outside my family and I just let you in. Because you were nice to me.' She laughed, low and bitter. 'How desperate must I have been? God, you must have thought you had it made.'

Anger rolled through his body, working its way up through his chest and finding its way out of his mouth before he could even think to censor his words.

'You talk about trust? If you trusted me one iota you'd listen to me. You'd let me explain. You'd trust me enough not to jump to the worst conclusion at the first sign of trouble.' Violet stepped back at the force of his words, and he wanted to feel bad about that but he couldn't find it in himself. 'How did you even find out about that story? Did you go hunting for a reason to put between us? Or did someone tip you off?'

The faint splash of pink that coloured her cheeks told him that he'd hit the mark. 'Who was it? Rose? Or another reporter?' The obvious truth slammed into him and he almost laughed at the ridiculousness of it. 'It was him, wasn't it? After everything he did to you, you still trust his word over mine.'

'I trust facts!' Violet shot back. 'How I found out doesn't matter – except that it wasn't from you. If you want my trust, you have to give me the truth.'

'How could I tell you this?' Tom asked. 'Violet, you've been hiding away here so long, so scared of what people might think or say, you don't even know what trust looks like any more. You wouldn't even talk to me about whether you were in a relationship! I was falling madly in love with you and I couldn't even say the words in case I spooked you. In case you jumped to exactly the conclusions you ran to today.'

'The right conclusions,' Violet countered, conveniently ignoring all his other points.

'No.' The anger faded, as fast as it had come, and all Tom was left with was that cold, hard certainty. 'You're wrong about me. I made a mistake ten years ago. But since I've come here the only mistake I've made was believing that you could move past *your* mistakes, your history, and find a future with me.' (Pembroke, 2015, pp160-161)

Fortune's June Bride by Allison Leigh

'Why wouldn't I be all right?'

'I don't know.' He yanked on Rusty's shirt and slammed the white cowboy hat on his head. 'You just saw the love of your life again.'

His vehemence had her blinking. 'He's not-'

'He didn't know who I was until Caitlyn, in her infinite good manners, started introducing everyone.'

Unease settled perilously closer to dread. 'He didn't-'

'-mention that you and I were *newlyweds*?' He air-quoted the word. 'Fortunately, he managed to avoid saying it outright. But he damned sure left everyone with the impression that we were together.'

She let go of the locket. And the ring. 'I'm sorry.'

'Caitlyn, no doubt, will mention the news to Brodie.' His voice was flat as he finished buttoning the shirt and flipped up the collar to pull on the string tie. 'It's only a matter of time before it gets to my parents.'

'And that has you all riled. That your parents might think we're...together.' After they'd spent two hours with them the evening before over tamales, while Galen had gone out of his way to treat her no differently than he'd treated his sister Delenay.

'I'm not riled.'

'Well, you're something!'...

Only a semblance of professional pride made her leave the trailer ahead of him. 'Galen, I'll explain what happened. There's no reason for your family to believe we're...involved.'

Particularly when he was making it abundantly clear that they were not. No matter what had happened between them over the past week.

'And the love of your life?' His lips were thin. 'He got the job, by the way. But it isn't in Chicago.'

Her stomach started to fall away.

'It's right here in Horseback Hollow.' He threw out his arm. (Leigh, 2015, pp186-187)

Rachel's Holiday by Marian Keyes

The previous examples are all 50,000 word category romances so in short romances like these, this function is usually covered by one chapter. Conversely, Rachel's Holiday is a 200,000 word women's popular fiction novel with romance as an element; hence this function is covered over a number of chapters and includes elements of falling out with her lover, disastrously getting together with another man, and relapsing into her drug addiction.

To my surprise, Josephine said baldly to Luke 'Did you love Rachel?' My guts clenched.

He didn't reply. Just sat very still, looking at the floor.

There was a long, tense unbearable pause. I held my breath. *Did* he love me?

I desperately wanted him to. He sat up and ran his hands through his long hair. I tensed for his answer and he took a breath before he spoke.

'No,' he said. And a part deep within me withered and died.

I shut my eyes from the pain.

It's not true, I forcefully reminded myself. He was mad about you, still is.

'No,' he said again.

All right, I thought, we heard you the first time, you don't have to rub it in.

'If she was the nice Rachel, the one who wasn't always off her face and smarming over those fashion assholes,' he said thoughtfully, 'then I would have loved her, no problem. No better woman.

'But that wasn't the case,' he added, 'and it's too late now.'

I stared at him. I could feel grief stamped on my face. He wouldn't look at me.

Josephine paused and looked at Luke. 'Coming here and doing what you've done today, it must have been very painful for you?'

'Yeah,' he mumbled. 'I am very...' he paused for a long time, 'sad.'

The word resonated in the air.

My mouth and throat felt full of something. Below my chest, I had a burning feeling, but my skin was goose-pimpled and cold.

Josephine announced the end of the session. Brigit turned and left without looking at me. Before Luke left he held my eyes for a very long time. I tried to read something in his. Contrition? Shame?

But there was nothing…

As soon as we both took our clothes off, which was an ordeal in itself, I instantly felt all the passion ebb away. I knew, I just *knew* that he'd gone right off me. I could almost smell his panic.

And I'd gone right off him too. He was all wrong. Too small. No matter what I felt about Luke, there was no denying that he had a fine body. In comparison, Chris was lacking in every department. And I mean *every*.

We were both too polite to call a halt to proceedings…

It felt very, very wrong to be penetrated by a penis that wasn't attached to Luke. But at least events were moving on and it would be over soon.

Wrong.

It lasted for ever…

And a long, long time later he stopped…with a slowing down and a marshmallowesque texture to his willy, that was nothing less than an admission of failure.

'Sorry, Rachel,' he muttered, not looking at me.

'It's OK,' I replied in an undertone, not looking at him either…

In full view of everyone in the pub, he chopped two gorgeous, fat lines on the formica table.

Fearfully, I looked around to see if anyone minded, but they didn't seem to.

He rolled up a tenner and neatly hoovered up one of the lines. The bigger, I noticed angrily.

And then it was my turn. My heart was already pounding and my head already lifting in joyous anticipation. I bent over the coke. It felt like a mystic moment.

But just as I was on the verge of sniffing, I suddenly heard Josephine's voice. 'You were killing yourself with drugs.

The Cloisters has shown you another way of living. You can be happy without drugs.'

I wavered. Tiernan looked at me quizzically.

You don't have to do this.

You can stop right now and no harm will have been done.

I hesitated. I'd learned so much in the Cloisters, made such progress with myself, admitted I was an addict and looked forward to a better, brighter, healthier, happier future. Did I want to throw it all away? Well, did I?

Well, did I?

I stared at the innocent-looking white powder, arranged in a little line on the table in front of me. I had nearly died because of it. Was it worth continuing?

Was it?

Yes!

I bent over my cocaine, my best friend, my saviour, my protector. And I inhaled deeply.

I woke up in hospital...

I stood in the baking street and pointlessly, powerlessly ached to be able to change things. I wanted to go back and make the past different. I wanted to be still living in New York, to never have left, to not have been an addict, to still be Luke's girlfriend.

I lingered for a while, half-hoping Luke would appear, half-hoping he wouldn't. Then I realized if anyone saw me they'd think I was a stalker, so I moved off.

At the end of the street, I stopped. I had to. Tears blurred my vision so much I was a danger to myself and to others. I leant up against a wall and I cried and cried and cried and cried. Mourning the past, mourning the other life I might have lived if things had been different. (Keyes, 1997, pp456-457, 539-540, 553-554, 606)

The recognition that fells the barrier

'In a scene or scenes the author represents the new information that will overcome the barrier.' (Regis, 2013, p36) For external conflicts / barriers here 'these impediments are removed or disregarded.' (ibid) The external factors are often simpler to resolve by a change in situation. But much more important to contemporary romance novels is 'an interior battle, in which case the recognition scene consists of the heroine understanding her own psyche better. In the course of the book she has learned to know herself and distinguish sound perceptions from unsound. She sees the hero clearly and realizes her love for him. Both what is recognized and when it is recognized vary enormously.' (Regis, 2013, p37) This enormous variation depends on the individual characters, their relationship history, drivers, childhood, vulnerabilities, goals and drivers. Again, as with the declaration scene(s) the placing of this isn't specified, according to Regis who explains that 'In an upbeat, rapidly-paced book, the recognition scene may be in the last few pages and lead directly to the ending. In a bitter-sweet, slower-paced book the recognition scene may be quite early, and the barrier, which eventually falls, does not do so quickly.' (ibid) Again, this allows for plenty of variation within the use, placing, impact and emotional punch of this element of a romance novel.

Their betrothal

'In a scene or scenes the hero asks the heroine to marry him and she accepts; or the heroine asks the hero, and he accepts.' (ibid) Regis adds that marriage isn't necessary in romance novels from the last twenty-five years of the twentieth century, 'as long as it is clear that heroine and hero will end up together.' (ibid) Similarly to how the placing of other elements of these eight essential elements of the romance novel impacts on the type of story, emotional impact and knock on effects otherwise, the splitting of the betrothal and acceptance scene similarly changes the novel's focus 'inward, to confront the internal barrier that prevents the proposal scene from also being an acceptance scene.' (Regis, 2013, p38) In other words, what emotional conflict does the hero/ heroine have that means s/he can't immediately accept the proposal? Exploring that in itself offers the romance author a rich seam of possibilities to mine.

So, even though these eight essential elements are, according to Regis, needed in a romance novel, they are far from a 'cheat sheet' or 'formula' to write the same story again and again, as romance critics would have us believe. Instead, they are a list of ingredients needed to bake a romance cake, but notably absent are any quantities, description of a method, or an order in which the elements should be combined, hence leaving the romance author happily free to use them however she wishes.

Books as products

Some authors get very snippy and defensive when talking about books as products and instead they say books are art, and that an author should write what her muse tells her to write.

Yes, they are art, but also they're entertainment and also a product. It is possible for something to be both a product and art at the same time. Or as Andy Warhol said: 'Being good in business is the most fascinating kind of art. Making money is art and working is art and good business is the best art.' Warhol, n.d.)

When a customer buys a product she's not really buying the product, she's buying a solution to a problem. When you buy a car you're not thinking about buying an engine, four seats, four wheels and some metal and glass; you're thinking about providing a solution to your personal mobility. Same with a book. Your reader isn't interested in buying the paper and the cover, it's the story inside she's really after. The problem a book answers is being bored, lacking entertainment, distraction, and a book should aim to provide that entertainment and distraction and escape.

In the next chapter I'll cover why readers come back again and again to enjoy romance books, so you can make sure to include those elements in your stories. I'm pretty sure they won't come as much of a surprise, and if you read the promotional text for any romance novel the same phrases and promises come up time and time again. This is intentional, because it's based on what readers want.

Genre vs formula

When anyone criticises romance books – and that's pretty often really – they often confuse the term formula with genre. Regis explains the difference clearly and far better than I could manage: '"Formula" denotes a subset of a genre. It is narrower than a genre. The elements of the genre are all present in the formula, but their range of possible embodiment has been constricted.' (Regis, 2013, p23)

Further fuel is added to the 'all romance novels are formulaic' fire by the use of line or category tip sheets. These are the guides publishers issue to describe the types of things required by each line or category. Because the tip sheets are specific about the requirements for any given formula, it makes books written to the tip sheet's specification, technically a formula. However, like most things involving words and not numbers, it's not quite that simple. Nora Roberts (and if anyone knows their romance onions, it's her) says that these tip sheets are the 'culture' of each series. (Mussell, in Regis, 2013, p24) Obviously, the formula / culture of that series still meets the broader requirements of the romance genre overall (as covered in the definitions earlier) but the different lines / categories, are a 'wholly contained subset of that larger genre' – of romance. (Regis, 2013, p24)

Taking Nora Roberts' view about these lines is a useful way of thinking about them; rather than being formulas (which has negative connotations) but instead the 'culture' of a line.

Coming back to my point earlier about romance novels being products just like anything else, let's imagine you're in a supermarket and you really want a ready meal. You browse to the right section and find there's a variety of different options: Italian, Chinese, Indian, traditional British. Each different line has its own standards and similarities – say spiciness, types of meal, sorts of carbs etc – but would you say that all Italian meals are the same? Would you look at the variety of Chinese ready meals on offer and conclude they were formulaic? Would you prefer the ready meals were all arranged alphabetically, regardless of line, so you could find a prawn dansak next to a pizza and some pilau rice? Or would you prefer them arranged, as they are, by country of origin, or line?

Let's imagine for one instance that romance novels are ready meals and that to aid the customer with her choices, rather than being presented with a mass of alphabetically listed romance books, they are arranged by lines, each line with their own word count, amount and presence of sexual content, extent of suspense in the plot, in a variety of time settings from medieval through contemporary to future, and to their geographical setting too.

Even though all the ready meals are very different, they're all prepared meals you can heat up and eat in a short amount of time. Similarly, all the romance books 'consists of books that have the eight essential elements of the core romance....Readers of a given line, therefore, know that they are not only getting a romance novel, but they are getting a romance novel of a certain kind.' (Regis, 2013, p157)

Because romance is driven by the characters, and one of its clear genre conventions is that it's about the developing relationship between the hero and heroine (or two of each) I think it's worth exploring what sort of ideals these are according to readers.

The ideal hero

Alan Boon is quoted in McAleer's 1999 book, *Passion's Fortune: The Story of Mills and Boon* describing 'what a romance hero ought to be – in accord with the "law of nature," he ought to be the "strongest male of the species" in order to attract females.' (McAleer in Regis, 2013, p158) The definition of what that strength means and how it expresses itself, has definitely changed gradually since the 1970s when the company started to focus on publishing romance. There's not time for a detailed discussion on that here, because this isn't a book about that, however, suffice it to say I've included some more contemporary definitions of what romance readers define as their ideal hero.

Sharon Kendrick, a prolific Mills and Boon author, with over 105 published books and over 25 million copies sold worldwide, explains, 'And you wouldn't want a short fat balding hero – women know too many men like that.' (in Flood, 2010) A sheik, Kendrick says, 'represents the ultimate female fantasy – dark, autocratic, completely powerful, outrageously chauvinistic' (ibid). In the same *Guardian* article, Penny Jordan adds, that a hero has 'obviously got to be sexy and high powered because they go together. And they always like them to be well off. But for me he has to have some interest in charity, to do something for the good,' and Yates adds that although her hero is 'still an alpha male, but he's maybe a little more willing to talk about things at times'. (ibid)

In Radway's study, *Reading the Romance*, the five most important qualities in a hero, as rated by the respondents are: intelligence, tenderness, sense of humour, strength and protectiveness.

This is all very good and well, but I find their descriptions during focus group interviews more interesting and useful as an author wanting to ensure my heroes live up to reader expectations. In Radway's study the women used phrases like 'strong but gentle,' 'masculine but caring,' 'protective of her and tender,' 'a he-man but a lover-boy too.' (Radway, 1991, p130)

From these it's apparent that female readers of romance want a man to be both the opposite of herself (the traditionally masculine elements) while also complementing her and supporting her (the more traditionally feminine elements).

In terms of big name publishers of romance, who know how to create heroes readers will want to return to again and again, 'the Mills & Boon hero remains a particular sort of man and not the kind real life is likely to deliver. He's dangerously sexy while also moral and loyal, a confident, charismatic alpha whose heart's desire is you.' (Oliver, 2015)

The ideal heroine

Mills and Boon author, Kendrick's heroines 'are not always beautiful, and like most women are plagued by insecurities. I'm not very good at writing high-powered career women. It could be because I haven't had a high-powered career myself. But if she's a barrister or a newspaper editor, it wouldn't really be feasible – I want her to be spending time with the hero. She tends to have to be flexible. And if she's a chambermaid, if she's sacked it's not the end of the world.' (in Flood, 2010)

I think that contemporary romances need heroines that reflect the modern woman and Penny Jordan agrees: 'I'm always interested in giving them interesting careers' and blowing the stereotype of the winsome heroine out of the water, Jordan adds, 'I want them to assert themselves when necessary.' (ibid) While Yates adds they should be 'feisty career women'.

But what about sexual experience? Barbara Cartland used to have a parade of young virgins in her romances, but they were historical so is it realistic to expect a heroine in a contemporary romance to be similarly chaste? Jordan, who sold over 100 million copies of her books worldwide for Mills and Boon says, she 'usually makes her heroine either a virgin, or inexperienced.' (ibid)

In the Radway study, Dot, the woman who writes newsletters recommending good romances to her fellow readers explains the 'romances she most values and recommends for her readers are those with "strong," "fiery" heroines who are capable of "defying the hero," softening him, showing him the value of loving and caring for another.' (Radway, 1991, p54) Again, this blasts out of the water the myth that heroines in romances are quivering women waiting around to be told what to do by the heroes. The romances I've read have all featured heroines with their own agency, their own will and more often than not, they stand up to the hero's demands.

Reading romances from the seventies and eighties, I was struck by how often the woman is 'possessed' or 'overpowered' by the man; that is the basis of the relationship goal at the end. However, in more modern romances, from the nineties onwards, it is increasingly based on a relationship of equals; man and woman with equal stakes in their love.

The Smithson women in *Reading the Romance* describe their favourite heroines as: extremely intelligent, spunky, independent and unique. (Radway, 1991, p101)

Contrary to most people's beliefs, Modern Mills and Boon heroines 'do not have to be winsome virgins longing for wedding bells – though that's still a perfectly good Mills & Boon plotline. They can be divorcees, single mothers and secret mistresses. They might even be the ones doing the seducing.' (Oliver, 2015)

Lubbock's law or point of view

Finally, before moving onto the next chapter, a word about this. It refers to Percy Lubbock, a literary critic who wrote *Craft of Fiction* in 1921 and he 'claimed that the best fiction was written from the heroine's point of view because it intensifies, emotionally, whatever is being told.' (in Regis,

2013, p158) Certainly, until the eighties, category romances from Mills and Boon only included the heroine's point of view. (Oliver, 2015) So the importance of Lubbock's law is likely less influential than thirty or so years ago. More contemporary romances have been told from both hero and heroine's points of view with perhaps a 40 / 60% split respectively. Since the 84% majority audience of romance is female, it makes sense to focus on a character she can identify with most. (RWA, 2014)

Things to remember
• Understanding what the majority of romance readers expect when reading a romance book means the author can choose consciously to ignore or abide by these expectations.

• The eight elements of a romance novel are useful when writing a category romance, where the story focuses on the romance, to ensure you cover all the parts the readers are expecting to see.

• Genre and formula are different.

• Knowing what readers expect in an ideal hero and heroine means you can ensure yours keep your readers returning to enjoy more of your books.

Things to consider
• Does knowing what romance readers expect from books change anything about how you'll write your next book?

• Does knowing these expectations make you want to write any of your already published books differently?

• Are some of your books more popular with readers than others? Could this be to do with reader expectations?

Things to do
• Read a romance novel and see if you can identify scenes related to the eight elements of a romance book. Consider if you've covered all of them in your latest book. Have you received feedback from beta readers that could be

about missing one or more of the elements out? They may not have described these elements in the same words but it should be clear which they're referring to.

•   Think about your hero and heroine (or hero and hero, or heroine and heroine) of your current work in progress and ask yourself if you've created them to be ideal in the view of romance readers? You don't have to have all the elements identified in every hero and heroine, but it's important to think about why they don't exhibit some of the characteristics, and explore that in your story.

CHAPTER 10 - Why women enjoy reading romance? How to give your readers customer delight moments and keep them coming back for more, or in marketing speak how to do 'relationship marketing' with your readers

Now I'll move onto the reasons why women enjoy romance so, once you understand this, you can make sure your stories do exactly what romance readers enjoy and then they will come back time and time again.

Why do you want readers to return again and again? Well, apart from leading to more sales, there's a whole area of marketing that focuses on this.

Relationship marketing.

You know the reward points you collect in supermarkets and other shops? That's relationship marketing.

I'm going to use a table to explain the key differences, and then give examples.

Key principles of transactional and relationship marketing

Transactional	Relationship
Focused on single sale	Focused on customer retention
Orientation on a product's features	Orientation is product benefits
Short time scale	Long time scale
Little emphasis on customer service	High customer service emphasis
Limited customer commitment	High customer commitment
Moderate customer contact	High customer contact
Quality is primary concern of production	Quality is the concern of all

(Christopher et al, 1991, p9)

An example of transactional marketing is selling one book to a customer. Let's say she's stumbled across your book in the Amazon rankings or the 'other customers bought this' section and she's one-clicked your book. Taking the principles for transactional marketing one at a time I'll explain how that applies to this one sale.

This is one sale. It's unlikely that the reader will come back and buy more of your books as a result of this transaction (unless you're a big author brand name, in which case I doubt you're reading this book).

Transactional sales focus on the features – remember FAB – features, advantage, benefit from earlier, these features are the most simplistic qualities of the book. Its setting, character types, maybe even the number of pages etc. Not very emotive for buying a book.

As it's one single sale, the timescale is short. The customer one-clicks, and has no further interaction with you as an author. Hence there's little (or no) emphasis on customer service. As a one time transaction you can't give anything other than the book itself because, as we said, she's moved onto another purchase by now.

All of the previous principles lead, unsurprisingly, to the reader having little commitment to you or your book. It was almost as if she bought it by accident simply based on a few factors. Because she has no relationship, or knowledge about you or your books, she's unlikely to have any sort of commitment to you either. There's no loyalty leading to her coming back for more books.

Moderate customer contact – she may Google you, check out your website and social media profiles – but it's probably pretty unlikely.

The quality aspects aren't really relevant to this example because they're more applicable to a product involving a series of different departments.

Relationship Marketing
If we move now to how it works with another purchase of a book but this time using relationship marketing principles.

The focus here isn't on just the one book sale, it's on retaining that reader to buy future books you write. Assuming you're planning to write more than one book, this is important. Remember the reward points, they're to encourage you to come back to the shop and buy more stuff. You want your readers to return and buy more of your books. Therefore you want to be trying to develop a relationship with them.

Rather than focusing on features, here you're focussing on benefits. The benefits your book gives to the product, as defined by what she values in your sort of books. See the earlier section for more explanation about benefits and how you can write a value statement.

Because you're focussing on developing a relationship, and that's not done in seconds, unsurprisingly, the focus is on long time-scales. You wouldn't think it was realistic to meet someone at a party you liked, and then suddenly become friends with her in seconds, would you? Neither should you expect to develop relationships with your customers (with a view to selling her more books) overnight either. Relationships take time to build.

As you're developing a relationship with the customers, you will inevitably do this through giving good customer service. This is more than simply selling the book (because probably they've bought the book from a third party vendor, like a book shop or online shop, rather than you personally). You can give good customer service by offering up your social media details in the book if the readers want to get in touch with you. You could give away an e-book if the reader signs up to your newsletter once they've read to the end. You could give the reader an opportunity to take part in a question and answer session or comment on your blog.

Unsurprisingly, all of these mean you're going to be having high customer contact through relationship marketing. With the internet, never before has it been easier for readers to engage with their favourite authors.

Ideas for developing relationships with your readers

• Join Facebook groups for your genre of books. Use it to share your interests about reading and writing, but don't promote yourself. Join in the conversation and you may be able to introduce readers in that group to your own books. Engage, engage, engage, not sell, sell, sell.

• Ask for some helpful, very engaged readers to beta read first drafts for you (or a draft you're happy to share before submitting it to publisher, agent, self publishing).

• Involve readers in certain details of your current work in progress – naming a character, fictional place, asking if any have similar experiences to your main characters you can ask for realistic details.

- Give away an e-book for everyone who signs up to your newsletter – post periodically when you have something new to say. Include specific content that's not available elsewhere so they feel special and there's a reason to sign up to the newsletter.

- Do book giveaways – physical books and e-books for competitions and to encourage people to comment on articles you've written and posted on the internet.

- Tell readers where you will be (festivals, conferences, libraries) and encourage them to meet you and get one of your books signed.

- Offer ARCs to some readers on the understanding that they should do their best to post a review on Amazon, Goodreads etc.

- Hold twitter chats monthly, using your own hashtag #askliamlivings for example where you'll respond to questions from readers about your books etc. Link the content of these back to the themes in your latest book.

- Newsletters – save special content for this. Don't just re-jig your blog content. Include snippets of stories you're working on. Add in deleted scenes from published words. Have little short stories with characters in published books. Don't set yourself up for a monthly newsletter and then be scrabbling around for content. You're better to send as and when you have something interesting to say. Make sure the newsletter has news in it, and not just a lot of not very much.

- Street teams – this is a closed Facebook group for fans of your books to talk to you and about your books. You could ask about naming characters, pose dilemmas about plots, or share snippets of works in progress and early cover reveals. The secret to this space is it must feel and look different from the other internet spaces you inhabit. It should be more intimate, more open and more focussed on your books, than perhaps a general Facebook update which may focus on your life more broadly. Your readers have joined the group to talk about your books. Make sure that's the place they can do it.

So those are some practical tactics you can use to develop ongoing relationships with your readers. I wouldn't expect you to do all of them, but it's worth working out what you have time to do and what you feel comfortable doing and then give those a try.

One of the aims of relationship marketing is of course to get readers returning to buy all your future books, but a by-product of it could also be lots of word of mouth praise about your books from readers to other readers; and that is much more powerful than any other type of review you can get. Readers trust other readers more than they trust a book critic or an author.

But why, in the age of information, the internet, online video streaming, is the novel still so popular?

DBC Pierre, winner of the Man Booker prize sums it up perfectly: 'a novel is not information...This is information: "She went to New York that summer." This is a story: "I melted in New York last summer."' (Pierre, 2016, p124)

Even though that is the first line of a highly regarded literary novel, *The Bell Jar* by Sylvia Plath, the distinction remains and popular genre fiction is absolutely not about imparting information; it is about storytelling.

Pierre also sums up perfectly the difference between enjoying a novel and other forms of entertainment: 'a breaker crashing over someone in a film is not the same as a breaker crashing over someone in a novel. A film crashes over someone else. A novel crashes over you.' (ibid)

Reading a novel is a solitary and much more immersive experience than other forms of entertainment.

This explains why, in an age full of information, connectivity, and sharing, the solitary experience of reading a novel remains popular, regardless of the medium through which it is enjoyed (e-reader, phone, tablet, paperback). Or, as DBC Pierre puts it, 'Let the information age tweet pictures of gnocchi. Find the shady tree, slip away. I rest my case.' (ibid)

To illustrate this I've included some 100 word openings of romance novels encapsulating Pierre's points:

The moment I set eyes on Jeremy West I knew I had to have him. I was sitting in Arabella's, watching a crowd of debs and other phonies undulating round the floor and thinking they were dancing, when suddenly the bamboo curtain was pushed aside and a blond man walked in and stood looking around for a waitress.

Even in the gloom with which Arabella's conceals its décor I could see that he had class – tall and lean, with one of those beautiful cheek-boned faces with long, dreamy eyes like Rudolph Nureyev. (*Octavia*, Jilly Cooper, p7)

Anne

September, 1945

The temperature hit ninety degrees the day she arrived. New York was steaming – an angry concrete animal caught unawares in an unseasonable hot spell. But she didn't mind the heat or the littered midway called Times Square. She thought New York was the most exciting city in the world.

The girl at the employment agency smiled and said, 'Aah, you're a cinch. Even with no experience. All the good secretaries are away in those big-paying defence jobs. But honest, honey, if I had your looks I'd head straight for John Powers or Conover.'

'Who are they?' Anne asked.

'They run the top modelling agencies in town...' (*Valley of the Dolls*, Jacqueline Susanne, p1)

Prologue

'Damnit,' she realized. 'I think I'm having a nervous breakdown.'

She looked around at the bed she was flung in. Her well-overdue-for-a-bath body was sprawled lethargically on the well-overdue-for-a-change sheets. Tissues, sodden and balled, littered the duvet. Gathering dust on her chest of drawers was an untouched arsenal of chocolate. Scattered on the floor were magazines she'd been unable to concentrate on. The television in the corner relentlessly delivered daytime viewing direct to her bed. Yep, nervous-breakdown territory all right.

But something was wrong. What was it?

'I always thought...' she tried. 'You know, I always expected...'

Abruptly she knew. 'I always thought it would be *nicer* than this...' (*Sushi for Beginners*, Marian Keyes, p1)

The man standing at the foot of the long staircase was one tall, dusty cowboy and looked entirely out of place standing on the polished wood floor in his boots and spurs and bat-wing chaps. A straw hat was pulled low over his forehead, but the moment he spotted her descending the long stairs, he swept it off to reveal thick waves of varying shades of chestnut. Yet it was the speculative gaze on his face that jarred Lilly Lockett the most and prompted her to lift her chin to a challenging tilt.

She halted two steps from where he stood with a gloved hand resting on the polished balustrade. 'Are you lost?' (*One Tall Dusty Cowboy*, Stella Bagwell, p7)

'Why is your face blue?'

Holly froze in shock. She had just opened the door to the apartment she'd expected to find empty. But instead of flicking on the lights in a vacant living room she'd walked in on lamps already blazing. And a shirtless man sitting in the center of the sofa. Reading a newspaper. A gorgeous brown-haired shirtless man was reading a newspaper.

'Why is your face blue?' he repeated. Broad shoulders peeked out over the newspaper he was holding.

Why is your face blue? Holly heard the individual words but couldn't put them together to understand them as a question. (*Her New York Billionaire*, Andrea Bolter, p7)

But why do women enjoy reading romance?

According to Janice Radway, as discovered from her extensive research with the Smithson women in the 1984, in America, the reasons can be categorised in three main areas:

1. as being compensatory (for experiences lacking in their real lives)
2. escape (in two senses of the word)
3. emotional experience – falling in love with the hero and experiencing the emotion of falling in love alongside the heroine. (Radway, 1991)

I hope you can see how, even in just 100 words, the previous extracts of romance novels fulfill at least one, if not all three, of these reasons Radway discovered. I'll explain each of these three areas in more detail so you can make sure you're writing your romance novels to fulfill them too.

Compensatory

Romance is *compensatory* literature. This basically means it makes up for experiences that the readers lack in their real lives.

Radway finds that it compensates readers in two ways: emotional and experiences of travel. In the first way, romance 'provides vicarious emotional nurturance by prompting identification between the reader and a fictional heroine whose identity as a woman is always confirmed by the romantic and sexual attentions of an ideal male. When she successfully imagines herself in the heroine's position, the typical romance reader can relax momentarily and permit herself to wallow in the rapture of being the center of a powerful and important individual's attention.' (Radway, 1991, p113) In other words, romance readers experience the feelings alongside the heroine, of falling in love with the hero. Whether or not this is actually compensating for not having that feeling in her real life is another matter. And more recent research on romance readers suggest that most are not single, but in fact in happy relationships, but when you experience such a wonderful feeling of falling in love, why wouldn't you want to relive it time and time again each time you read a romance?

Why not indeed.

So as a romance author you need to make the most of the emotions, show and tell us how the heroine and hero feel as they gradually fall in love.

You can do this in lots of ways and the tips from the Mills and Boon authors about sex scenes in the *Guardian* article bear repeating here. There are only so many different ways one can describe sex, but a romance reader (as opposed to an erotica reader) wants to travel on the emotional journey with your characters, so rather than describing the in and the out of what is physically happening, you can do that, but a romance reader is likely to be more interested in the emotions that go with the sex. What are the characters feeling before the sex, the anticipation? What does it do to their feelings after the sex, how does it change their love for one another? (in Flood, 2010)

The second way Radway says, romance is compensatory, is that it 'fills a woman's mental world with the varied details of simulated travel and permits her to converse imaginatively with adults from a broad spectrum of social space.' (Radway, 1991, p113)

I think this is now less important since this study took place in 1984, as well as being less relevant for countries outside of America, for a few reasons: travel has become much more affordable since the time of the study; more European people have passports and travel outside of their country than even now Americans do. However, that's not to minimise the importance of *setting* in a romance novel. How often have you seen a cover with a beautiful setting and simply bought it because it allowed you to *travel by book*, rather than having to get on a plane? In addition to this, 'travelling by book' aspect, Radway also asserts that learning about other locations means 'a woman can indulge herself by engaging in an activity that makes her feel good and simultaneously congratulate herself for acting to improve her awareness of the world by learning through books.' (ibid)

Again, with the advent of the internet, I'm sure this is less important, but the attraction of an exotic setting and rich descriptions, to a romance still bears thinking about when you're writing your next one. The amount of setting description varies depending on the type of romance you're writing. A category romance of 50,000 words doesn't have much spare wordage for long descriptions, unless they're relevant to the romantic mood of the scene. A candlelit dinner, a star filled sky, a sunset over mountains in an exotic location. These details are worth spending a few words on, so your reader gets the experience of feeling like she's travelled, all from the comfort of her armchair.

However, a women's popular fiction novel of 90,000 to 150,000 words has much more wordage to include descriptions of far flung islands, the food they eat, the village in which the story is set, to give the story real atmosphere and make your reader feel as if she's been to that island.

Similarly with a historical romance, a certain appeal of reading stories like those is about the nostalgia, the memories of times past, so take the opportunity to evoke that with descriptions of things from that era.

However, as with everything, it must be done in moderation. Remember, readers have come to your romance books for the story, for the romance between two people, not for a travelogue or a history lesson. So only include enough setting and description to evoke the atmosphere and don't let it get in the way of telling a damned good romance story!

Escape

This is a very important reason why women read romance. You've only got to read the covers of some popular romance novels to see how often the word 'escape' crops up. The Smithton readers explain escape in a number of ways:

'They are light reading – escape literature – I can put down and pick up effortlessly.

Everyone is always under so much pressure. They like books that let them escape.

I guess I feel there is enough "reality" in the world and reading is a means of escape for me.

Because it is an Escape (sic), and we can dream and pretend that it is our life.

I'm able to escape the harsh world for a few hours a day.

They always seem an escape and they usually turn out the way you wish life really was.' (Radway, 1991, p88)

But importantly, romance novels allow the readers to escape in two different ways – that are different from other forms of entertainment such as watching TV:
1. because reading requires concentration and is a solitary activity, unlike other forms of entertainment.
2. it differs from other types of reading, because romance is specifically written in such a way as to be effortless to read – which I'll come onto shortly.

But what are the two ways in which romance provides its readers with escape?

Radway finds that romance reading as 'an activity, it so engages their attention that it enables them to deny their physical presence in an environment associated with responsibilities that are acutely felt and occasionally experienced as too onerous to bear.

Reading, in this sense, connotes a free space where they feel liberated from the need to perform duties that they otherwise willingly accept as their own.' (Radway, 1991, p93)

Bearing in mind this study took place in the early eighties, using a group of housewives from the Midwest of America, that this aspect of escape will have moved from work around the house, to any sort of work outside of the home that women are now engaged in almost as much as men. You've only to look at women reading books on their commute to work, or their lunch breaks, to see this purpose hasn't changed even if its setting has. By ensuring your romance is effortless to read, by making it clear and simple (which contrary to popular belief is actually harder than writing something complex and long) you're supporting the reader to escape effortlessly into your world. Write what you mean and mean what you write. I'll come onto this effortless to read style shortly in more detail.

The second way in which romance provides an escape is that 'by carefully choosing stories that make them feel particularly happy, they escape figuratively into a fairy tale where a heroine's similar needs are adequately met. As a result they vicariously attend to their own requirements as individuals who require emotional sustenance and solicitude.' (ibid) This differs from other genres of popular fiction since the genre rules associated with romance do indeed assure the reader that all will end well, hence fulfilling this second, equally important aspect of *escape* a romance novel provides.

One of the Smithton women explains that she occasionally gives herself 'a very special treat' when she's 'tired of housework.' 'I take the whole day off,' she said, 'to read.' (Radway, 1991, p91) Fiction reading is a particularly solitary leisure pursuit unlike others, which supports it being something that is a treat for an individual, rather than something shared with others (husband, partner etc).

For the great majority of romance readers, a happy ever after or a happy for now is key to their enjoyment of the genre. *It's the certainty that all will end well that makes romance such a comforting and happy reading experience.* It maybe sounds obvious but writing a romance that ends well, and has a happy journey along the way is very important to the readers of the genre. That doesn't mean you can't have lots of conflict and obstacles for your main characters to overcome, but the reader should enjoy spending time with your characters and watching their romance blossom gradually as they overcome obstacles. All the while, in the certainty that all will end well.

Escapist yet realistic - This escapist lark is a bit more complex than it may at first seem though.

Despite romance readers knowing that the characters and what happens are 'fairy tales or fantasies [they] also insist that they contain accurate information about the real world' hence the importance about the setting as I've already covered. (Radway, 1991, p109)

How is it possible to have both escapist fairy tales grounded in reality? Radway explains this comes from readers separating the plot and setting.

The romance plot is an escapist fantasy, yet the setting itself is realistic.

Readers explain that romance isn't like reality, that it's a fairy tale because 'reality is neither as just nor as happy as the romances would have it. Rewards do not always accrue to the good nor are events consistently resolved without ambiguity in the real world. A romance is a fantasy, they believe, because it portrays people who are happier and better than real individuals and because events occur as the women wish they would in day-to-day existence.' (ibid)

Because, after all, why would you read to escape if the fiction was exactly the same as real life in all its complex, unjust, uncertain messiness? This brings us back to one of the criticisms so often levelled at romance – that it's formulaic.

I've already explained that within the plot of romance there are countless variations, but overall, we must remember that the happy ever after, the certainty that the hero and heroine (or two heroes, or two heroines) will end up together, is as certain as Tuesday following Monday, and that, for romance readers, is the appeal of the genre.

Forget this at your peril.

Make sure your characters are better than real people – more interesting, more in all ways – and that their emotions are happier and also sadder than in real life. It's exactly *this exaggeration* that readers are wanting in their romance. And also, make sure your plots are just. You know how in soap operas the evil character always, eventually, gets their comeuppance? It's the same in romance.

By ensuring your romance book's setting is realistic, believable and something readers can relate to (even if it's in a spaceship in the year 2300) the plot and the characters will be more easily accepted and enjoyed as fantasy, exaggerated and therefore escapist.

Emotional experience

Because romance as a genre is about the developing relationship between two main characters, and now we know about the compensatory role of romance in terms of experiencing emotions through the heroine, it will come as no surprise that emotion is one of the main reasons that readers enjoy romance. If, as an author, you can nail the emotions the characters are experiencing, you'll have readers returning time and time again for more of the same but different.

The Smithton women asserted repeatedly that they prefer the 'one woman – one man' kind of book. (ibid) This again links back to the development of the relationship throughout the story. If you have characters hopping in and out of bed with a variety of partners, the development of the one main relationship will inevitably become confused and slowed. This confusion is something readers of romantic fiction will enjoy, with its broader canvas, longer word count, larger cast of characters, but for a category romance with word count limits, it must focus on two people's relationship.

Radway explains 'what they [readers] want to experience above all else is the hero's protective concern and tender regard for the heroine. It matters little whether that care and attention are detailed in general terms or presented as overtly sexual as long as they are extensively described. (Radway, 1991, p105) In other words, you don't need to have explicit sex scenes for this emotion from the hero to the heroine to be experienced by the reader, you just need to make sure it's there. On. The. Page.

Radway finds that 'romance reading seems to be valued primarily because it provides an occasion for them [readers] to experience good feelings. Those feelings appear to be remarkably close to the erotic anticipation, excitement, and contentment prompted when any individual is the object of another's total attention. In effect, romance reading provides a vicarious experience of emotional nurturance and erotic anticipation and excitation.' (ibid) Therefore it's no coincidence that Mills and Boon's popular True Love line of category romances is described as follows: 'Celebrate true love with heart-felt stories of tender romance, from the rush of falling in love, to the joy a new baby can bring, and the focus on the emotional heart of a relationship' (M&B website, n.d.)

So why do readers come back to read romance novels again and again?

It's a bit like why eating one square of chocolate is never enough...The happiness experienced by readers from reading romance, as I've already covered, 'is not only second-hand experience,' (as in it's not from the reader's own experiences, but through reading about characters in a fictional setting) 'but temporary as well.' (Radway, 1991, p117) This is where Radway gets a bit more cynical, but realistic too.

She explains that by 'resting satisfied with this form of vicarious pleasure, the romance reader may do nothing to transform her actual situation which itself gave rise to the need to seek out such pleasure in the first place.' (ibid) In other words if you're reading to escape an unsatisfactory job, home life or friendships, by reading, the escape it gives you allows you to put off actually doing anything about the dissatisfaction you feel about your real life.

Although this is true, I think it ignores the fact that so much dissatisfaction in life isn't big enough to change things for. The Smithton housewives describe taking the children to school, cleaning the house, making the husband's lunch and although that isn't necessarily the ideal thing they'd want to do with their lives, they are content overall, so romance provides them with temporary respite. Plus, who really lives a life only filled with endless tracts of amazing, fulfilling, exciting experiences? Exactly!

So, and this is where Radway becomes quite cynical, 'Consumption of one temporarily satisfying romance will lead in that case to the need and desire for another...at the same time its very ephemerality may guarantee a perpetual desire to repeat the experience. Consumption, in short, might result only in future consumption.' (Radway, 1991, p118) So by giving readers what they want from reading a romance, you will keep your readers returning for more and more and more.

And, as an aside, in terms of addiction, being addicted to romance novels is pretty harmless when compared to alcohol, drug or sex addiction, don't you think?

Delivering reader satisfaction

To deliver reader satisfaction time and time again, a romance author needs to include the factors I've already covered: emotion, romance, character development.

Another important aspect of a romance is how the characters must learn and be changed by the end of the story. This was expressed by the Smithton women in Radway's study as: 'Generally there are two people who come together for one reason or another, grow to love each other and work together solving problems along the way – united for a purpose.' In addition a romance is described as 'a man and woman meeting, the growing awareness, the culmination of the love – whether it's going to jell or if it's going to fall apart – but they [the heroine and the hero] have recognized that they have fallen in love' (Radway, 1991, p65)

I watched a documentary about ABBA where Pete Waterman – who's had 22 number one singles in the UK, so he knows a thing or two about pop music – said the thing about an ABBA song is that it *delivers you the song*. Specifically, he says, 'They told you what the song was, and why it was written. There was no airy fairyness about it. It was like – this is what the story is and here's the pay-off. They [ABBA] understood that and they delivered that every single time. So when you heard an ABBA record...you never really listened to it. It was...almost like musac, it was perfect.' (BBC, 1993)

Now, compare that with some prog rock band, from the same time period like "The Ancient: Giants Under The Sun" by Yes about whether a lamb cries out before it's shot dead and the movement of the head, and consider whether you know what that song is about? Indeed, what's going on in *that* song?

Doubtful.

Popular genre fiction is exactly the same as Waterman's description of an ABBA song. *It delivers the reader the story*. It should tell you who it's about, how they feel, what happens, and how it ends. And in the same way that Waterman says you never really listen to an ABBA song, reading a romance novel – if it's written right – feels like you're not reading at all; it's effortless and it immerses you in the fictional world without you needing to think. I'll come onto how romance does that next.

Have you ever read to the end of a piece of beautifully written literature and wondered quite what it was all about? I know I have

Writing style

Although it seems counter-intuitive, writing simple, clear words is actually harder than writing long complex bewildering phrases. 'Shorter is better. Many famous writers of the past were experts at saying what they meant in very few words, and simple, often one-syllable words at that. Milton and Shakespeare were deft users of simple words...' (King, 2009, p4)

As Strunk and White summarise in their 20 million selling *The Elements of Style, the beauty of brevity*: 'Vigorous writing is concise. A sentence should contain no unnecessary words, a paragraph no unnecessary sentences, for the same reason that a drawing should have no unnecessary lines and a machine no unnecessary parts. This requires not that the writer make all his sentences short, or that he avoid all detail and treat his subjects only in outline, but that every word tell.' (in King, 2009, p129)

I think it's interesting and important that the quote uses the word 'tell' for what every word must do. There's an awful lot of stock put into the 'show don't tell' brigade in fiction, and having discussed this with less experienced writers and tried to explain it to authors of manuscripts I've been appraising, I think it's one of the most over-used trite and over-simplistic phrases in fiction writing. And, having read a lot of romance, I also think it's basically twaddle in terms of genre fiction.

For those who may not be familiar with what 'show don't tell' means, the general wisdom is that one should *show* the emotions and character traits of the characters through their actions and dialogue rather than telling the reader. This is all good and well as a rule of thumb, however it ignores the fact that there's another sort of telling: summarising, where one skips past uninteresting or unimportant events rather than showing them on the page as they actually happen.

Only, the thing about romance is that it tends to *tell* the emotions and character traits *as well as* showing them through the dialogue and actions. But, and this will come against the received wisdom, especially from the 'show don't tell' brigade, that's not necessarily A Bad Thing. The main attraction of reading romance, and why it's such a popular genre, is that it's effortless to read, and can enable the reader to escape into a new world and escape from her real life for the time she's reading.

In order to achieve that effortless reading experience and such deep escape, the romance needs to be written in a way that doesn't require much, if any interpretation by the reader. There should be no need for the romance reader to work out what's happening or what something means. The simple act of reading should be enough to follow the story and enter the fictional world it's describing. Remember Pete Waterman's comments about not needing to listen to an ABBA song? This is the same but for reading.

Unlike literary fiction, where the reader is expected to infer meaning from the text, to deal with ambiguity and lack of clarity, a romance book's words are there to *deliver the reader the story*: the emotions, the plot and the characters. Janice Radway sums this up: 'Romances further obviate the need for self-conscious interpretation by almost never assuming that their readers are capable of inferring meaning, drawing conclusions, or supplying "frames." Typically, after describing a verbal response that any reader can infer is prompted by anger, the writer confides redundantly, "she was angry." Repetition is the rule, not the exception, governing these novels.' (Radway, 1991, p196)

It seems from that previous quote that Radway is criticising romance for using this technique, but she shortly explains that isn't the case and explains that this type of fiction can only be judged to be of lamentable quality 'if one agrees with Henry James that all fiction ought to demonstrate with subtlety rather than tell overtly.' (Radway, 1991, p196) Perhaps we have Henry James to blame for the 'show don't tell brigade' nowadays!

And why does romance use these techniques in its writing? Usually reading – unlike for instance watching a TV show, where the product is complete and you simply passively consume it by watching it – is completed by the act of reading. Reading is a much more open-ended act than simply watching a TV show or a film. But by employing these techniques romances 'guarantee that even the laziest and most unimaginative reader will know not only what is occurring but what it means as well.' (ibid) In other words, romance says what it means and it means what it says. Although Radway's previous quote is pretty snippy and aimed at romance readers, I, and evidently millions of other romance readers too – don't think there's anything wrong with having the ambiguity taken out of fiction and being able to simply enjoy a story at its face value.

Coming from a communications background, I learned that the main purpose of written communication was to share a message with its reader. Hence the importance of plain, concise and clear English. If the reader, after completing the text by reading it, is still none the wiser about what it's about, then the text has failed. End of.

For romance, since we've learned that it's a marketing-led genre from a content point of view – plots, characters, settings etc – it's therefore not that surprising to learn, romance is also a communications and marketing-led genre from a writing style perspective too. In other words, the writing style romance uses to convey the content is clear and concise.

Turning it on its head, it wouldn't make sense that a genre, so led by the desires and need of its voracious readers, would present the customers with what they desired, but only once they'd foraged through dense thickets of vague adjectives, confusing similes accompanied by opaque dialogue and abstract thoughts. It would be a bit like handing a customer a new smart phone and the instructions booklet being in a filing cabinet of hand written index cards.

Because usually the act of reading itself, completes the production of the story – in other words for most non popular genre fiction the reader has to do some work herself in interpreting and understanding ambiguity – this sort of reading often feels like hard work. OK, so some people enjoy this type of reading. But the great majority of readers don't want more work in their fiction after they've done a day's work, and a commute and made dinner and put the children to bed and fed the cats. Most readers simply want reading to be a pleasure and effortless and to enable them to *escape*. Remember how important escape is for romance readers, in both the senses of the word?

Have you ever wondered why romance readers rarely talk about the beautiful phrases or prose they use in their books and are much more likely to talk about the characters and how they found their made-for-each-other love? This is because in romance genre fiction, the writers and readers 'understand the purpose of the text to be the romantic tale itself,' rather than the purple prose used in the text. (Radway, 1991, p198)

And as I've had told to me so many times, story is king, story is king, story is king. In other words, even if it's a beautiful paragraph, passage, scene, if it's not necessary for the story, then it should go. As Radway describes it, 'the activities of writing and reading as a storytelling cycle.' (ibid) Rather than writing words for the sake of writing the words...And I'm sure we all know what it's like reading those sort of books!

Isaac Asimov describes two ways of writing fiction in his essay "The Mosaic and the Plate Glass" which illustrates the difference between placing the emphasis on *the beauty of the words* and putting an emphasis on *conveying the story*.

Imagine you are looking out of a window at what is happening in the street; this scene in the street represents the story you're trying to tell, but the different windows you look through represent the type of writing employed to tell the story.

'In one way [of writing] you pay more attention to the language itself than to the events you are describing. You are anxious to write colourfully...The effort to be colorful and yet to avoid the cliché is difficult...If you succeed, you have written poetically. You have written with style. Everyone admires you – at least, everyone with pretensions to literary taste. And yet, though the phrases may be memorable, though the swing of the sentences may be grand, though the moods and emotions may be effectively evoked – the story may be just a little bit hard to understand. Such writing is like a glorious mosaic built up out of pieces of colored glass. It may be a gorgeous spectacle and wonderful to look at, but if you're interested in seeing what's going on in the street, you're going to have a little trouble seeing through the mosaic.' (Asimov, 1987, p20-21)

The second way of writing, he describes, is the one used in popular genre fiction, particularly romantic fiction; here the story, that is to say, what is happening in the scene in the street behind the window, is much more important than the window itself. In this way of writing, 'words and phrases are chosen not for their freshness and novelty, or for their unexpected ability to evoke a mood, but simply for their ability to describe what is going on without themselves getting in the way. Everything is subordinate to clarity. It is this kind of writing in which the direct sentence is preferred to the involved subordinate clause, the familiar word to the unfamiliar word, the short word to the long word...All things being equal, you plump for the direct, the familiar, the short...' (ibid) This means this way of writing is easy to read, 'effortless' – as Radway describes it in her study with voracious romance readers.

Using Asimov's analogy, in this latter way of writing, you can see what is happening through the window, in the street beyond 'with absolute clarity...Ideally you're not even aware of the writing.' (Asimov, 1987, p22) In contrast to looking through a beautiful mosaic glass, here the 'writing might be compared to plate glass in a window. You can see exactly what's going on in the street and you're not aware of the glass...' (ibid)

Although it may seem that this easy reading is easier to write, as I've explained using communications and plain English theory, it's actually just as hard, if not harder than writing in an ornate, deliberately opaque fashion. Asimov sums it up perfectly: 'Writing in such a fashion that the writing is unnoticeable, that the events described pass directly into your brain as though you were experiencing them yourself, is a difficult and a necessary art.' (Asmiov, 1987, p22-23)

When writing a romance you want your readers to read it and feel as if they were experiencing the emotions, the story, knowing the characters for themselves.

The last point about the reader feeling as if she is experiencing the events themselves is very important for romance. The emotional journey is one of the main reasons readers enjoy romance books; this clear effortless writing style ensures she believes she's experiencing the events of the story herself: falling in love with the hero, overcoming the barriers to the romance alongside the heroine, travelling to the setting of the story. Writing clearly puts these front and centre of the reading experience, rather than being obscured by difficult to read phrases and sentence structures.

To illustrate this effortless to read writing style, I'll use extracts from one popular romance author from a variety of different time periods. I've deliberately picked an author who's no longer alive to prevent offending anyone. Penny Jordan was a very popular category romance author, writing 187 books and selling more than 100 million copies worldwide during a 30 plus year career with Mills and Boon. And, it's also worth adding, for the avoidance of doubt, I'm using these extracts to illustrate the points I've made above, and not to criticise the quality of the writing.

My comments on the text are in italics and square brackets.

The Six-Month Marriage by Penny Jordan

Perhaps it was a trick of the moonlight, but his face seemed oddly white and drawn, his eyes burning as though he had looked into the fires of hell. [*into the fires of hell – Is this a tired cliché, or actually a really simple clear way of conveying what his eyes look like because readers can immediately imagine this?*]

'Stand back from the edge Sapphire, and I'll thrown you down a rope.'

She was too bemused to question how he had got there, simply obeying the commands he shouted down to her, feeling the coarse fibre of the rope bite into her waist as Blake hauled her back up the quarry face, until she was lying flat on her back, on the ice-cold grass, breathing in great gulps of air, like a landed fish. [*bemused – that's telling us how she feels, but what's the alternative, a furrowed brow, some long internal monologue to show us how she's bemused, or just tell us. coarse fibre of the rope bite into her waist – very sensory, as soon as someone writes 'bite' you imagine a bite. Like a landed fish – is this a cliché – I'm sure more literary critics would insist it is, but really, it gets the job done. We imagine her gulping in the air. Do we need it as well as the previous few words? It could do without it, but to be honest I think it gives some more colour to the scene.*]

Blake's fingers tugged at the knotted rope, unfastening it from around her. His head bent over his self-imposed task, Sapphire resisted the urge to reach out and stroke the thick darkness, but she couldn't restrain the brief quiver tensing her body when she remembered how they had made love. [*tugged – clear anxious typed verb showing how worried Blake is to save her. Restrain the brief quiver – inappropriate at this point? Maybe, but this is romance, it's fiction, it's a fantasy. The fact that the hero is rescuing the heroine means this is a critical and really romantic*] *moment, so yes, let's have her remembering how they'd made love before. We welcome the melodrama in romance and that's often what more literary corners seem to criticise.]*

'Keep still,' Blake's voice was terse, his hands clinically detached as they examined her body. 'Nothing seems to be broken...Come on, I'd better get you back and alert the rest of the team.' As she stood up Sapphire saw that his mouth was compressed, his eyes darkly bitter as they studied her... *[clinically detached – so he's not feeling the romance, he's concentrating on rescuing her, making sure she's safe – powerful in only a few words. Mouth was compressed – that's showing us how he may feel, but then we're absolutely clear how he feels, as his eyes are darkly bitter. He's bitter for her doing something so stupid to risk her life. Studied her – he's remote, removed from the situation, not simply looking at her.]*

'In view of his ailing health I suppose you mean,' Sapphire cut in sarcastically, only to be silenced by Blake's brusque, 'Not now Sapphire. You realise your father's practically frantic with worry, to say nothing of how I felt...' *[Lots of telling of emotions in this paragraph, but honestly, who cares? It's a great high drama romance scene. Sarcastically – so we're told how she interrupts him. We could have managed without that from simply what she says, but to be honest the sarcastically makes it absolutely clear, means we know exactly how she feels, so why not include it? This is built on with a brusque. Blake isn't upset with her for what she's done, he's angry with her for risking her life, for meaning he may have lost her, and all that's clarified in a simple, brusquely tacked before his dialogue. It's like a little arrow at the side of the road in a journey telling you the right way to go.]*

'And how did you feel Blake?' she asked bitterly, suddenly furiously and intensely angry, the adrenalin flowing fiercely along her veins. (Penny Jordan, 1985, *The Six-Month Marriage*, pp172-173) *[Again, lots of telling of emotions here too, but without the bitterly, furiously and intensely angry, how do we know exactly how she feels? She could cry, or stamp her foot, or shout, but there's only so many times a character can do that. And* the way Jordan adds the adverbs after the dialogue and then describes adrenaline flowing along her veins, it combines both simple telling to get the message across, with some beautiful more literary imagery that also really bangs home how the character feels. This sort of over the top description of emotions in this way, is pretty typical of romance novels. Why? Because readers want to experience the emotions the characters feel. And a really simple way to do that is to show the reader what the characters say, but also tell her what she's feeling, and on top of that add some imagery so she can see how the character feels too. Jordan does all of this brilliantly in this short last sentence of this extract.]

Yesterday's Echoes, Penny Jordan

She was shaking violently now, barely aware of the small, frantic voice inside urging her to be more cautious, but suddenly she needed to vent her emotions, her bitterness, to tell Jake Lucas how she felt, how she hurt. *[shaking violently – do we need the violently afterwards? We could have done without it, but by adding it, the reader has a more unhinged view of the heroine's actions. There's some repetition of words in this section – her is repeated three times, how is repeated twice – which are often criticised in more literary circles, but here, the repetition makes it absolutely clear how the heroine feels and it reflects the jumbled physical shaking of the heroine in her jumbled shaky thoughts.]*

It was as though the injustice of his accusation, coming on top of all that she was already suffering, had driven everything but her need to defend herself from it out of her mind. *[injustice, accusation, suffering, defend – all strong words. Although quite broad and unspecific, they immediately conjure up immediately feelings, emotions in the reader so she experiences the emotions with the character.]*

'How *could* I love him after what he did to me? The way he forced himself on me...the way he ruined my life...?' *[the power of the ellipsis. A lot can be said in dialogue by the gaps left. We know how painful it is for her to describe what happened after he forced himself on her because she fades the sentence off...]*

She was crying now, raising her hands to dash the tears away impatiently as the rage continued to burn through her, fuelling the hot outburst of everything she had kept locked inside herself for so long. [crying is definitely showing us how she feels, but very shortly afterwards we're told she is impatient, and raging, and the 'hot' although general is simple and conveys her emotions quickly and simply.]

'Ritchie forced himself on you…?'

The sharp question sliced through her hysteria, shocking her into silence. [sharp, sliced, hysteria, shocking – short, active, simple words. Without needing a metaphor Jordan has said that the question sliced through her hysteria like a knife, but she doesn't use the extra words. The reader knows what she means. Who hasn't described a question or some words as slicing through you?]

She was shivering, ice-cold with shock and reaction, Rosie realised shakily, as the icy disbelief in Jake Lucas's voice cut through the heat of her emotional outburst. [shivering, ice-cold, shakily, icy disbelief – these are effectively repeating the same concepts in the same sentence, but it's used for effect and contrasts well with the heat of her outburst.]

'Are you trying to claim that Ritchie raped you?' he demanded acidly. 'Because if so…' [acidly – another adverb to tell us how he says the dialogue. But short of another stare, or him throwing something, or jumping into the man's head for some internal dialogue, this adverb achieves it all, simply, quickly, and lets us get back onto dialogue, before quickly returning to her thoughts and emotions. Remember Lubbock's law – here it is in action.]

Nausea clawed at her stomach. She had to stretch out an arm towards the wall of the house to support herself and yet, despite the terror, the fear rising up inside her, despite the vivid image etched on her brain of the way this man had stood and watched her as she lay rigid on his aunt and uncle's bed, her still only youthfully developed breasts partly revealed to him, her body numb with panic and shock but her brain, her emotions rawly vulnerable to the contempt, the disgust with which he was regarding her, Rosie suddenly knew that if she backed down now, if she allowed him to use her vulnerability and pain against her so that he could reject the truth, she would suffer for that weakness for the rest of her life. She had made that mistake once; she wasn't going to make it a second time. (Penny Jordan, *Yesterday's Echoes*, pp74-75, 1993) *[Nausea is telling us how she felt, but the clawed is simple and visual to give us more emotion on top of the nausea. The second sentence is very long, but effectively broken up by commas. It's a clever way to show the building of pace and the jumbling of the character's thoughts. Read the second sentence and it's like the gallop of a horse, or the clatter of a train as it moves from one section to the next between commas. Terror, fear, vivid image, etched, numb, panic, shock, disgust, vulnerability, pain, suffer, weakness – all emotions we're told in this sentence. Imagine trying to show us all of those. It would have taken a whole chapter and who's got time for that? Among these emotions is a very powerful image of her on the bed, with 'only youthfully developed breasts partly revealed to him' so Jordan is throwing this in so the reader sees that and experiences the emotions with the character, as well as the emotions that have been told.]*

A Secret Disgrace by Penny Jordan

Louise walked towards the open double doors into the bedroom. *[Note the lack of description of the doors and the bedroom. A reader knows what they look like, we don't need a three paragraph long description of the bedroom – unless there's blood on the bed – we'd much rather get to the action and the emotions.]*

She had almost walked through them when she heard Caesar saying casually, 'You've never told me. How was it that you were so sure I was Oliver's father? That you were able to state categorically to your grandfather that I was?' *[she heard Caesar saying – that's a perception filter. We're already in 'her' head, so the author could have written 'Caesar said casually,' but contrary to what I've been told before perception filters don't matter. And to be honest, now I hardly notice them. Casually –*

telling us how Caesar feels without a lot of eye rolling or hands lazily hanging by his sides and other such filler.]

She couldn't move, transfixed on the spot as though physically constrained there, was able only to turn and look at Caesar as he looked at her. He neither knew nor cared how cruel and hurtful he was being, but she cared – *she* cared a great deal, Louise recognised. *[couldn't move, transfixed on the spot, physically constrained there – these are all doing the same thing, so could some of them go? Jordan is making it very clear how physical this sticking feels for the character, hence repeating it three times in one sentence. It's like a double take, so the reader really gets it too. Cared, cruel, hurtful – telling how he feels. She cared is repeated – for emphasis, but next to each other, some would say it's not wonderfully phrased. Who notices that among all the other drama of the scene?]*

She knew what he was thinking, and what he was implying. Of course she did. How arrogant he was to stand there, inferring that she had selected him from a number of men who might have fathered Oliver and judging her for it when the reality was… *[This is the character thinking through what to do next, hence the repetition. Arrogant – we're told how she feels about him, and so should we, for the avoidance of doubt.]*

Out of nowhere a fierce wave of pride and anger swept through her, overwhelming caution and self-protection, and before she could stop herself she heard herself telling him fiercely, 'I knew because it could not have been anyone else but you. I knew that you were Oliver's father because you were the only man who could be.' (Penny Jordan, *A Secret Disgrace*, pp135-136, 2012) *[fierce wave, swept through – a great visual image for the emotions that she tells us – pride, anger, caution, self-protection and then we're told she speaks 'fiercely' because that's more emotional and simpler than having the character bunch her fists or stamp her feet to show us how she feels. Plus, why bother with drab descriptions of what she's doing like that, when we've just had a fierce wave of emotion sweeping through her, which is far more interesting and visual to read.]*

How do readers feel about this 'effortless' writing style to romance?

Well, in *Reading the Romance*, one of the Smithton women describes well-written romances, making it clear 'that she believes that success in writing has nothing to do with elegant phrasing or the quality of perfection but is a function of the uniqueness of the characters and events intended by the most familiar of linguistic signs.' (Radway, 1991, p189)

In other words, she isn't interested in beautiful words, but the things that these words stand for – the characters and the plot. The reader 'seems to judge writing solely on the basis of the efficiency with which it gets its job done, that is, tells the story.' (ibid)

Janice Radway goes on, saying readers 'come to the romantic text, then, with the understanding that its language is there to describe, in simple and unambiguous terms, events that for all intents and purposes were "completed" just before the fictional narrator described them...In addition, these women also believe that the author herself provided the meaning of the story for her readers by expressing it in words.

They believe that meaning is in the words only waiting to be found. Reading is not a self-conscious, productive process in which they collaborate with the author, but an act of discovery during which they glean from her information about people, places, and events not themselves in the book.' (Radway, 1991, p190)

This sort of reading, unlike more literary fiction, where the reader is required to interpret, fill in the gaps, to complete the text itself by reading it, is more like watching TV in terms of it being easy. It's more involved than watching TV because the reader is required to see the images, to interpret for herself what descriptions like independent, intelligent, handsome, forthright mean to her, but it is nowhere nearly as involved or challenging as that required from readers of more literary fiction.

Through this *effortless* writing style, the romance novel is *delivering the story* to the reader in an unambiguous way, just like an ABBA song, delivers itself to the listener, as Pete Waterman describes.

Why is this important to know as romance authors?

If we focus on the characters, the emotions, telling the story, and forget the purple prose, we're doing what the readers want. Anything you write that feels self-consciously like writing, rather than simply delivering the story, warrants a second look. Ask yourself if it's necessary, if it's clear, and if it could be simplified to focus on the important story elements as defined by the readers.

Structure – this is an important element to bear in mind when writing your romances because not only is the writing style and type of words used in romance different from more literary fiction, but also the story structure differs. Similarly to how a more intellectual or high-brow film has a different structure from a romantic comedy, or other more commercial films.

Story structure can easily be broken into three acts. The first act is the introduction to the world. At the end of this act is the inciting event – the thing that sets the rest of the story on its way. Act two is the main body of the story during which the protagonist goes through a number of events with conflicts and challenges, until the third act. In the third act the tension declines and the issues and story threads are concluded, with no new ones being started. (Harper, 2017)

Although a literary fiction story would still typically follow the three act story structure – it is simply the basic blocks of a story's beginning, middle and end – what happens in the second act, or the main block of the story, will differ.

In a less commercial, more literary novel, the series of conflicts will vary in intensity and type and then in the final act there will be a lowering of tension and conflict as issues are resolved. But there will not be a marked 'moment of ritual death' or 'oh sh*t moment' and neither will the conflicts build in intensity towards the end of the middle of the story. The ending will then either be downbeat or upbeat depending on the sort of novel; usually both with a quite open ending. In short, this sort of fiction is more realistic and life-like without a discernible pattern to the conflict's growing intensity to a climax.

Jenny Harper plots this in her diagram: (Harper, 2017)

THE 'LITERARY' NOVEL STRUCTURE

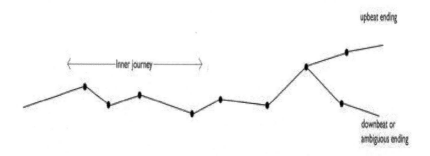

If this model was applied to a romance, it would mean a more unremarkable journey of the relationship's development and a point at which the characters were together, followed by them being together with not much tension to keep them apart, before their story simply ended, happily or unhappily. Sounds like a bit of a let down, doesn't it?

In a romance, the characters will go through a series of events, challenges, internal conflicts related to their emotions and past and external conflicts in relation to the situation they are in (time period, location, social structures). Here, these conflicts escalate in tension and size, becoming more difficult as the story progresses, until they lead to a peak of conflict, or the moment of ritual death, or the 'oh shit' moment. At this point it appears that all is lost, the hero and heroine can never be together, their difficulties and differences are insurmountable and all will end badly. And then, moving into the third act, the conflict is resolved, the hero and heroine are together, and they are seen building or living in their happy ever after together.

THE 'COMMERCIAL' NOVEL STRUCTURE

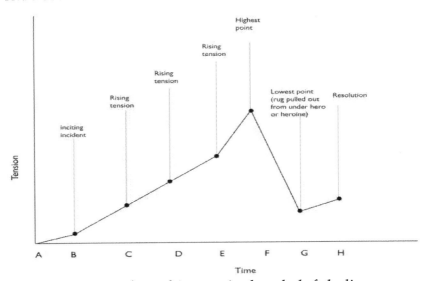

Jenny Harper plots this too in her helpful diagram: (Harper, 2017)

Being aware of this means romance authors can knowingly ensure their stories build to a peak of tension, gradually adding more and more drama and conflict as the characters want to be together but can't be for a whole host of external and emotional reasons.

How to ensure your stories will have your readers coming back time and time again for each new story

We've seen that romance as a genre is marketing-led in terms of how it takes its cues from readers' wants and needs. Publishers use categories to steer new stories along the lines they know readers will enjoy – semi-programmed issue.

Publishers and agents will seek new authors and books on the basis of books they've already published and that they know will work with readers. Some publishers use fully-programmed issue to sell their books based on a subscription model, ensuring each story sticks to the 'culture' as Nora Roberts describes it, of that line and is therefore highly likely to meet customers subscribing to that line's needs.

So how does an author use techniques and tools to use the same marketing-led approach to her books? If you think this means you're compromising your creative freedom, that's your prerogative. I am not suggesting you write a story exactly like a bestselling novel in your genre, I'm suggesting you get feedback on your writing, at whatever stage you feel comfortable, and use that to influence the final product. You, as the author, of course, always have the final discretion about whether to take the advice or not. And in my experience, this is a matter of crowd sourcing.

Similarly to if you read the reviews on a hotel and one person complains about the food, and everyone else says the food is wonderful, you take the complainer's comments with a pinch of salt. In the same way, if one beta reader tells you that your heroine isn't strong enough but the other three love her, then she's probably fine. But if three readers say she's a bit weak and wishy washy, then you need to take some action, revising the draft before it's published.

To involve your readers in the development of your books, you need to engage them. Engagement and relationship building doesn't happen overnight. It takes time. I've already listed some ways you can engage your readers.

To gather readers for your drafts, develop an email list for people to sign up to, making sure you're compliant with data protection rules obviously. Through this you can put out calls for people to read early drafts of your work. Have a sign up to your newsletter button on your website or at the end of your self published books. Offer a free e-book for people who sign up.

There are roughly two kinds of early readers: beta readers and alpha readers.

Beta readers are the people, usually not authors, who can read the story and give you comments about the pace, the characters, the setting, the romance and conflicts within the story. You're not wanting comments about spelling punctuation and grammar, you want these people to read your manuscript as if it were a published novel and give you their opinions. As a reader. Just like the Smithton readers Janice Radway spoke to, readers don't tend to care much about the writing style, they are much more interested on characters, plot, romance, conflict, emotions. You want comments on these aspects from your readers, not spelling and grammar issues, that's what an editor is for and if you're self publishing you can pay someone to fix that.

An alpha reader is someone you send the first draft to, either as you've finished it, including spelling and punctuation errors, or literally as you write each chapter. This is a very privileged position because it is right at the story's infancy, but it also allows big mistakes to be fixed before you've spent too much time tinkering with other parts. Say, for example the main conflict between your hero and heroine isn't big enough or deep enough to keep the story going for 50,000 words, and could, essentially be worked out over a cup of tea, then you have a big problem. Or your hero or heroine aren't very sympathetic or likeable characters. Isn't it better to know that sooner rather than after you've written the story during which the unsympathetic hero and heroine get together on page six and then spend the rest of the story arguing, which isn't proper conflict?

Things to remember
- Women read romance for: escape from their day-to-day life and into a fairytale world where emotional needs are met (in addition to or instead of how they're met in real life); to compensate for the travel they can't experience in real life, and to compensate for emotions they may or may not experience in real life (love, passion, sensuality); to experience a deeply emotional journey by falling in love with the hero and identifying with the heroine.
- Romance novels should be effortless to read and say what they mean and mean what they say. Remember the reasons above, if your readers are fighting to understand what is happening it'll affect how well the above points are experienced from the readers' perspective.
- Structure of romance novels builds gradually as the story progresses, with tension and conflict building to a peak where the reader believes the happy ever after is in jeopardy, but then it is resolved, with the tension falling and the conflicts being resolved for the hero and heroine to be together in their happy ever after. Ignore this structure at your peril as a romance author because part of the genre's expectations is a happy ever after that is earned after a building period of tension. Do you want readers to think your romance was unstructured and unsatisfying to read?
- Relationship marketing – ways to engage readers in an ongoing relationship with you and your books. Use some of these to build an audience.
- A good way to engage readers in an ongoing relationship with you, plus giving you a steer if your story meets reader expectations and ticks the boxes for why they read romance, is to ask readers to alpha and beta read your stories before they're submitted to be published.

174

Things to consider

- If you've read a romance book that's not been very enjoyable, was it because it failed on one or more of the reasons why women read romance? How could it have been improved?

- When you have periods of your life that are really stressful or unpleasant, think about the sort of books / entertainment you enjoy. Remember this for when you're writing your next escapist romance.

- When you've finished a romance novel you've really enjoyed, what are the things that stick in your mind about it? The characters? The emotions they felt? The sensual scenes? The setting? The way the author wrote certain passages?

- Think about how you currently get feedback on your novels. If you don't receive feedback until your editor / publisher receives it, what sort of things do they usually want you to change? Could you imagine involving readers at an earlier stage of your novel writing? At what stage would you be comfortable to involve readers? If you feel uncomfortable about involving readers in this way, think about the main reasons why that is, and what it would take to overcome them.

Things to do

- Look online for books similar in genre to your own and pick one with the highest star rating on Amazon or Goodreads. Buy a copy and read it, first as a reader, enjoying the story and letting it wash around you. Then re-read it, as an author, make notes on how the setting gives you a sense of really being there, how you can escape a dull day in Droitwich or a rainy day in Reading by reading a few chapters of the book. Look at how the author shows and tells the emotions of the characters, what words are used, does it, now you're re-reading it, feel a bit melodramatic, or over the top? How do you feel when you re-read these emotional passages? Read from a clarity perspective – how easy is the book to read? Did you have to go back to certain sections and read them again to make sense of what was happening, or could you simply read on as it all made sense easily? Plot out the rising tension points of the story, mark where the 'oh sh*t' moment is, when all seems lost and the happy ever after is in jeopardy. How did you feel reading that the first time?

• Look through the reviews of your own books and try to identify any readers who have reviewed all or most of your books, for good or bad – if it's constructive and not 'the postman delivered it when I was out and it was wet when I arrived home.' Try to find these readers elsewhere online and contact a few of them. Say you've noticed they review most of your books and you wondered if they'd be happy to give you feedback on your future books before they're published. The worst they can say is no. Be clear you don't want feedback on spelling and grammar, that's what editors are for, explain it's about the characters, the emotions, the story itself, how it makes them feel and how it can be improved to be like one of their five star books. Offer them a free e-book or paperback when it's published. This feedback from readers is gold dust.

CHAPTER 11 - Identifying your target reader

I've talked quite a lot about making sure your book and the way you promote it is focussed on your target reader, but I'm aware that I've not yet told you how to actually find her. When I was researching comparator publishers for the publishing company that had commissioned me to produce a marketing strategy, I developed a step by step way to do this by desk research – in other words Googling things. Since then I've read around the subject online and have used bits of D Blank's 2017 and C Yardley's 2015 models with my own ideas to list below exactly how to find your target reader all from the comfort of your own home.

Before we get into the detail of that, just a little reminder why you'd want to identify your target reader.

By knowing who your target reader is you can make sure you promote your book in the places she hangs out online and in person. This is promotion and using social media in a clever and targeted way, rather than scattergun. You can also ensure the messages you use to promote your book are targeted and positioned to really interest her and be more likely to induce her to buy your book. This is STP – segmenting, targeting, positioning, we covered in an earlier chapter.

Here's the step by step guide, as described by Dan Blank 2017, and I've added a bit more explanation to it too.

1. Find five to ten comparable books that have been published within the last few years. You're looking for books that are similar to yours – in terms of theme / setting / type of characters etc. And make sure you're not picking books that

are much more successful than yours is, it's about the books being similar if you were describing yours to a publisher, agent or friend. Don't be too modest, but also don't be too big headed. A good way to start this process is to look up your book on Amazon and see what other customers who bought it also purchased. Also, look within your sub genre on Amazon for similar books – similar covers, similar settings, similar concepts. Really check the other books to see if they are actual comparable books, or if it just looks like they are. You're only interested in genuinely comparable books.

2.   On Amazon read all the reviews for the five to ten comparable books you've found. Take notice of common themes / phrases / comments. You can even copy bits of the reviews into a separate document. You're looking for patterns and similarities. If everyone loved the ending, find out what that was about. If the hero divided opinions, look into what he was like and what reviews are saying about him.

3.   Repeat this for Goodreads using the same five to ten books. Often the reviews will be different across the two platforms. Again, looking for similarities and patterns in feedback.

4.   Now you have a list of the authors of these comparable books, Google them. Check out their websites and find their social media profiles too. Putting 'Liam Livings Twitter' into Google will bring up that social media platform. Ditto for Facebook etc. Make a note of which social media platforms these authors are on, and which ones they're not using.

5.   Enter the names of the comparable authors into Google and add: fans, reader group, book blog. Do it as three separate searches.

6.   These searches will lead you to forums and other places where the fans of those authors hang out. Look at what they're discussing, what they love, what they don't like – general interests and book related interests. You should also be able to find out how often they read, what books they recommend to each other. Take part, join in the debate if you want, but don't say you're an author because that may not go down well. If you prefer, just look and don't touch. Remember, you're here for research. Make a note of what the readers like, don't like, how they find out about new books, where they hang out online.

7.   After checking out the social media of these authors, look at the readers of these authors. Check out the readers now in more detail – look at their profiles, what they post about, the pictures they share, what they comment on, what they talk about – books and wider interests, where do they live, what sort of age group are they, what is their gender, politics, etc. This may feel like online stalking, but if it's online, then it's there to be looked at. Some people will have their social media profiles only viewable by friends, but most people's are open for all to see.

8.   Work through the different social media platforms – Twitter, Facebook, Instagram, etc and look at what sort of things the comparable authors share, post about, pictures. Look at which other authors these ones mention in their posts. Check out other authors these ones follow – a good way to find out other authors in your genre.

9.   Write all of this down so you are building up a picture of the places comparable authors hang out, what their readers are interested in talking about online, which social media platforms are most used, least used.

10. Now make connections with these authors, asking for help to reach similar readers to theirs (because remember your books are comparable) or directly reach out to the readers you find there. If you're connecting with readers do it as another fan for that type of book, rather than being all 'buy my book, it's the same'. You can connect using a direct email, a video message, turning up in person to an event where these readers will be and just engage with them, ask them for help to reach other similar readers of that type of book – don't sell to them, at events – talk to the audience one to one before the talk itself, network with the other speakers.

11. Review the separate document you've been writing with details about comparable authors and their fans. From this you should now have a good idea about what *your* typical readers look like. You can use this information to ensure your marketing communications (anything that communicates with readers about your books) speak most attractively and compellingly to your readers, and that you're hanging about in the same places (online and in real life) as these readers. (Blank, 2017)

Things to remember
- Finding out where your readers hang out in real life and online is the single best way to make sure your marketing efforts are well targeted and have as little wastage as possible.
- If you're an author you'll probably want to spend more time writing than marketing, so this method means your marketing efforts are more likely to result in sales than a broader more scatter gun approach.
- Something with high wastage would be putting a billboard advertising your book next to a motorway. Millions of people would drive past it, but likely only a small proportion would be interested in your book to buy it. Plus, that's a very expensive way to promote.

• However, if you find out that your readers are interested in baking cakes and tend to often be retired or semi-retired, attending local Women's Institute meetings, or going to village fêtes to sell your books, or looking in Facebook groups about baking and interacting there, is a much more targeted way to reach your readers.

Things to consider

• Look at other authors in your genre with big names, and see how they behave online. Which social media platforms do they use? Which ones don't they use? What do they post about? How often are they online?

• Look at publishers' social media accounts and analyse how they interact with readers. What do they post about? How do they encourage readers to respond, to engage with them?

• Are there some big name authors who clearly don't run their own social media platforms? How can you tell? What sort of reader engagement do they get?

Things to do

• Work through the step by step process and at the end you should have a detailed report for yourself covering the demographic profile of your readers.

• Now you have this, you can make sure everything else you do in terms of marketing speaks directly to your readers. Don't work hard, work smart!

CHAPTER 12 - Ideas for a book marketing campaign

Now you've written your book, you've made sure it's on trend, it ticks all the boxes as far as readers are concerned, you've researched where your readers are both online and in person, and now you want to launch your book into the world. Below, I've included a list of ways you can do this. I would suggest you don't try to do all of them, otherwise you'll do nothing but marketing for about six months, and I would suggest you pick a few from this list to write a marketing campaign that is congruent with your brand, and your publishers.

Author events

In a world in which people can buy books at the click of a button on their smartphone, an event needs to be more than just about the book. It needs to have a social element. If you pitch the event as something of a party, with drinks and nibbles, and possibly hold it in a bar or club, you're more likely to attract people than if it's simply an opportunity to buy the book.

If a bar isn't your brand, then hold it in a café over tea and cakes. Think about what your readers would enjoy from a book launch event.

Of course you should also ensure that your book is front and centre at the event, so you can include a reading of your book – pick an extract that sums up the book but that works out of context and will have the audience needing to buy the book to hear how it continues. Include an opportunity to sign the book too. You could talk about how the idea for the book came about, who's helped you with it along the way etc.

Make sure there's an opportunity to buy copies of the book – and some of your back catalogue if you want. If you need to sell tickets for the book launch, make the price low, say £5 and be clear that the book will be on sale at the event for less than it is available online, again to encourage readers to come to the event.

Ask some book bloggers to the event too, get them to report on the launch afterwards and you could hold a giveaway of a few copies for a competition you'd run in advance, drawing the winner at the book launch event.

Similarly to how, even with online music streaming and the ability to have your whole music library in your pocket, the live music scene has never been stronger, sociable, live ways for people to connect over a shared love of books, will always work.

Independent book shops

Large chain book shops can tend to be difficult to get into, but if you're lucky enough to have an independent book shop nearby, approach them and ask if they'd be happy to host a book launch. Make sure you have a concept or topic to the launch and link it back to an important theme in your book. This could be friendship and asking everyone to bring a friend to the launch, nostalgia and ask everyone to bring their favourite book from childhood, food and ask everyone to bring a favourite home-made recipe to the launch. Include some extra added value at the event on top of just being able to buy the book. If your book is about a woman giving up her job to open a cupcake business, give away cupcakes with every copy of your book purchased. If your book is set in a particular time period, dress up in costume from that period, and provide photo opportunities for people to take with you.

Think about holding this with other authors in the similar genre as you; it takes away the pressure of having few people attending. You can share promotion in advance and hopefully encourage each other's readers to try a new author's books.

Online events

If you can't afford to have an in person event, holding an online one can be a great way of engaging with readers all around the world.

The go live function on Facebook allows you to broadcast yourself by a video. Having a Facebook party at a designated time, and taking questions, posting links to music, pictures of virtual food you're eating, all gives the impression of being at a real party, without the cost of doing so, and the added advantage of worldwide reach.

Host a question and answer session online. Use a specific hashtag on Twitter and say you'll take questions on that hashtag at a designated time. Ask other authors to join in too if they write similar books to you. Post on social media that you're having an open blog week, and you'll blog about anything your readers want you to (within reason) and then post the blogs daily in the following week, using lots of social media activity to direct people back to the blog for comments. Make sure you include blurb and buy links to your new book at the end of each blog post. Theme the posts around something in your book – loss, love, first relationships, differences between now and 1940s, clothes from the time period your book is set in.

Traditional media

This is TV, radio, magazines, newspapers. When pitching yourself to these traditional media you need to remember they are news outlets and not just a repository for adverts. When you try to sell yourself you need to have a *story* to sell and it must be more than just 'I have a new book out'.

When preparing for a media interview, whether it's radio, TV or even in a magazine or newspaper, it's a good idea to have in the back of your mind what three to five messages you want to get across about yourself and your book. That way if you're asked random questions you can steer the conversation back to sharing your key messages. If you're asked something you don't want to answer, simply bring the conversation back to something you do want to talk about. If your book is linked to something that's very current you'll stand a better chance of getting space in the traditional media schedules.

When working with a publicist, you need her to work for you and not the other way around. You will know your book and author brand far better than she will. Help her to agree the key messages you want to get across in media interviews and tell her the pitfalls you're worried about being asked, so she can prepare some objection handling lines for you. There are plenty of useful phrases for taking control of the conversation and avoiding awkward questions. Just watch politicians being interviewed!

Online marketing

Realistically, this will be the way most authors do the majority of their promotion. Social media is social and not primarily for promotions, however, if you mix up your usual sociable posts with some promotion that will not annoy your followers.

The best sort of promotion on social media is not an advert as such, but a post that links something current with your book. For example, during summer, people are looking for an escapist beach read, so you could promote your escapist romance with a picture of the cover and some text to explain how your book will be perfect for beach reading.

Conversely, your book may be something warm and cosy to curl up with on a winter evening, so post a picture of the cover, some text that explains why your book is perfect for a winter evening, and then the buy links for the main places (Amazon universal link that takes the person to the Amazon in their country, so you don't make the post too long).

These sort of posts on social media are more likely to result in sales because they aren't viewed as adverts as such because they're giving the reader more than a message to simply 'buy my book' which is what a bad advert does. A post in this way is essentially an advert, but you've not had to pay to place it in a magazine, or pay for having it designed, you can do all that yourself in a social media post.

Remember to DRIP (Differentiate, Reinforce, Inform, Persuade) in all your promotional posts on social media. Link back to current events, trends, and mention your book's escapism, travel to another land, emotions, rather than how long it is and the basic plot. They can read that by clicking on the book blurb. These posts should feel as if you are personally recommending the book to that individual person through social media, rather than being a blanket 'buy my book' statement.

To make sure you catch different time zones you can use social media scheduling software. Tweet Deck or Hootsuite allows you to log in once or twice a week and schedule your posts throughout the day. This means you can spend an hour or so twice a week to post a mixture of promotional posts, as described, as well as what are called safe posts directing people to content on your blog.

A safe post is one that draws people's attention to something that's already published, and you're therefore deemed to be happy with, on your website. If you post a blog and then post the link to it on Twitter and Facebook, unless the people are subscribed to your blog it's pretty unlikely they'll first, see the social media post, and secondly then read the blog. However, if you post the blog live and then schedule four to six safe tweets / Facebook posts with a short piece of text about the blog, and a shortened link to the full post, that increases your chances of people seeing it. Hootsuite has a link shortening tool, so you pick which social media platforms you want to post to (I use Facebook and Twitter because they're my preferred platforms), compose the text, paste a link to your blog post which is shortened, and then either post at a specific time or at a random time. Posting at a specific time is useful if your content is related to a specific day or time, such as world book day, or a release of a book, but otherwise using random scheduling is good to spread the posts around during the week and make the most of capturing differing time zones.

Using this technique helps increase traffic to your website because by posting numerous times with the same link to a blog, you're increasing the number of people who can and will click on the link. This is why it's important to make sure your website is an effective shop window for your books, so once on your website they can browse to find out what books you've written, what others think of your books and sign up for a newsletter etc.

Is a blog tour a good idea?

A blog tour is an online tour of a variety of other blogs, each where you talk about your new book. So on Monday you could be on one review blog being interviewed about the characters, Tuesday you're on a fellow author's blog talking about the book's inspiration, Wednesday you're on another review blog explaining your writing routine for the story etc.

A blog tour takes a lot of time to organise, write the content and then to tell everyone you've done it. You can pay companies to organise it for you, but you've still got to write the content, which also takes time. I once wrote 10% of the word count of the book I was promoting on a blog tour and sold very few books during that quarter. Some authors always have a blog tour, others say it's not worth the time and they'd prefer to write the next book. Without doubt it is a way of telling your readers you have a new book out. Is it worth having a twenty-five stop tour each requiring a separate blog post of 500 words on a different aspect of your book? Possibly not...

An alternative to a blog tour is to post some interesting social media posts as I've described above with buy links and the book cover.

However, if you want to try a blog tour here's a few tips I've picked up from other authors, review blogs and my own experience:

1. Keep the tour short and targeted. Make sure you only approach blogs that review your type of books, and that have good number of page views each week – you're aiming for thousands here not hundreds. There's no point writing a wonderful interview for a blog that only has tens of page views each week. I would suggest no more than five stops on the blog tour. I've seen blog tours taking fifteen to twenty different places, and when you read the comments it's the same people commenting to win a free e-book on every blog. Everyone else has lost the will to read any more posts or follow the blog to its next destination. One approach which is very short is to have all the guest posts scheduled to appear on the day the book comes out. This means any sales will be on that one day, making it more likely your book will climb the sales charts, and therefore gain visibility on Amazon.

2. Keep the content special. Don't just post blurb and covers on these targeted blogs. Readers can see that anywhere, they want special insights into the book. Some suggestions that are special and usually popular with readers: character interviews, the story behind why you wrote the book, deleted scenes, discussion about the themes / issues in the book (make sure it's more than just rehashing what the blurb says, really get into the issues).

3. Keep the content concise. I used to write 1500 word blog posts for guest spots. There's a lot of research that suggests that people have short attention spans and skim read a lot of what they see online. Try to limit your blog posts to

400 – 500 words, and then at the end include the blurb, cover and buy links.

Give-aways – do they work?

There's so much free online content and so many free e-books that in my experience e-book giveaways don't really do much in terms of attracting new readers or much of a buzz.

A paperback giveaway is more likely to result in attracting more readers, because if it's a new book, there's no other way a reader can get the book for free.

Working together in groups of authors who write similar type books can work with giveaways, so you pool resources, and can cross-share readers who like one author and encourage them to start reading a similar one.

Networks and engagement

Use your author networks to promote your books, especially if they write similar books to yours. Have guest spots on each other's blogs, do online chats for more than one author on a topic you can both discuss, have a book launch at a book shop or library with two to three similar authors.

Things to remember

• A book launch is important and so you should try to use all the learning from this book about being targeted and reaching your readers in the right place.

• However, you shouldn't try to do all the things I've listed in the book launch list. Pick a few that you think are doable by yourself, with your publisher's help if appropriate, and then see how it goes.

• If certain things don't go so well this time, change it for the next book launch. Trying different ways to promote yourself and your books is a great way to work out what is best for you and your readers.

Things to consider

• Most authors don't enjoy selling but if done right, promoting your books isn't about you and your book, but about the readers. Make your promotional posts / tweets / blogs etc, all about the reader and why she's going to enjoy your book as much as another reader who said 'x y z' about it.

• If you think about engaging with readers rather than selling to them, the selling will feel much more natural and less forced. Once you've developed a bit of a relationship with some readers, it's then more acceptable to share a new cover of the book, rather than simply saying you have a book out and they should buy it. Sharing the cover and asking readers to comment on it, still tells them you have a new book out, but the post itself isn't about that.

Things to do

• For your next book that's out, write down a book launch plan. A few headings based on the list in this chapter. Decide which parts you're going to do, and then do it.

• Make sure every time you communicate with readers you DRIP.

• Make the posts engaging, ask questions, ask readers to share.

• Enjoy it. Be at one with marketing as you are with writing.

CHAPTER 13 - The role of the publisher

If you're published by one of the big five publishers, and you're a big enough name to them, you may be lucky enough to have a publicist assigned to help you with promotion. Lucky you! They can help promote you in the right places to reach the right readers for your book. Work with them, not against them. This should be a partnership, not a battle. It is, after all, your career as a writer and your book, which only you know best. However, the publicist has been employed to help you so take their advice about how to promote yourself. It would be worth discussing a publicity / marketing plan together.

Ask questions like:
- Which communications channels (different types of communication – social media, blogs, radio, TV, magazines etc) are you going to be using to reach your audience?
- What sort of publicity plans did they come up with for similar authors in your publishing house?
- How do they understand what your brand is as an author?
- What words would they use to describe your books and you as an author? Make sure they get this right otherwise you could end up in a village hall in Ventnor when you'd be much better off going to a fashion show in Fulham.

However, if you're not a big name, or if you don't have a publishing contract with one of the big publishers, it's likely you'll have to do most of the marketing yourself. In which case I've covered that in the earlier sections of the book.

Even big publishers that print books all over the world don't always have individual marketing plans and publicists for their authors; there are simply too many different authors. Plus, if the brand of the publisher is generally more prominent than the author's name, it's unlikely you'll be assigned much bespoke marketing resource other than the distribution of your books through shops, online and any direct to reader subscription models they may have. These, in themselves are great in terms of a marketing and aren't to be sniffed at. But you'll still have to do the marketing to make *your books*, *your name* stand out from the dozens of other books in a similar genre that publisher prints every month. And that's what I've tried to cover in this book.

Check the publishing contract about what it says in terms of marketing the publisher will carry out. As well as agreeing to distribute to the usual sales channels (online and in shops) there may be details of marketing tactics they'll use to promote your books. Smaller publishers are often completely silent about what marketing efforts they'll put in, which means, yep, you guessed it, it's all down to the author. If your publisher is essentially only going to provide a cover, an editor and distribute your book to the sales channels (most of which except book shops anyone can have access too) then ask yourself if it's worth giving away the majority of your royalties for this. Would you prefer to pay for the production costs yourself and then retain all the royalties? The latter option means you're an author as well as a publisher, and for some, that's not a road they want to go down, but for others it allows them complete creative control in terms of content, covers, distribution, promotion, publishing schedule etc.

CHAPTER 14 - Don't Panic – a pick and choose to do list for the overwhelmed romance author

I've covered a lot of ground in this book and probably for most, much of it will have included explanation of new words and exploration of different ways of doing things.

The most important thing to remember is that this book is about giving you a *structured way* to make *decisions* about your writing career as a romance author, rather than a scattergun approach.

I'm not expecting anyone to do *everything* in this book – it wouldn't be possible even if you wanted to, because you'd have to stop writing and only do marketing for the best part of a few months. Remember, you're an author first, and as part of that, you need to market yourself and your books.

Write first – remember without the product (the book) there's nothing to promote; there's only so long you can start building your brand and anticipating an audience if you have nothing to give them to read!

You may have already done some of the exercises I've listed at the end of most chapters, but if not, now you've read the whole book, I'd suggest you go back to the start and have a go at some of the exercises. I've listed some more practical things for you to do at the end of this chapter. And you'll be pleased to know that most of it simply involves sitting at a computer, looking at things online (remember that desk research aka Googling) and writing. OK, so it's not writing fiction, it's writing ideas, findings, things to do, but it's still writing. It's not like I'm asking you to do an oil change on a twelve year old Ford Mondeo!

The three main things I really want you to take away from this book are:

1. As a modern author, marketing and not just promotion, is your own responsibility so take ownership of it as you do your writing and it's easy to move to a marketing-led approach to your writing.
2. All these tools and techniques I've described in this book only require you to sit at a computer, sometimes researching online, and write down ideas, plans, things to do. And then for you to do them.
3. Marketing is not a magical dark art, it is, at its simplest, working out what customers want and selling it to them for a profit. And who doesn't want to hear from happy readers who've loved our books?

Have a look at this list below and pick one to do now. Yes, you! Yes, now, if you don't mind!

Once you start, you'll realise how much you know about your own books and the rest...well that's what the internet is for. Just remember to work through methodically, using the tools and techniques I've described and even if you don't get it perfect, it'll be much more strategic and targeted than jumping straight to 'let's do more Twitter' or whatever tactic you decide without considering what you're trying to achieve first.

Here's a list of things you could do now you've read this book:

*   Do some desk research as described in Chapter 4: look at customer feedback on your books, customer feedback on comparator books similar to yours. Look at how those authors interact with their readers, what their branding is like – on their websites, on their books etc. Use this info to refine your online branding. Use this info to shape the idea for your next book.

- Write a marketing strategy for WHAT you're going to do to market your products using the headings in Chapter 6. And then, while you're on a roll, write a marketing plan for the HOW you're going to deliver the marketing strategy, based on what you read in Chapter 7.
- Work through the marketing mix for your latest book – promotion, price, product, place as described in Chapter 3. If you self publish it is very important to consider each new book as a new product with its own marketing mix. If you're traditionally published it's still worth going through this thought process to help you decide on the bits you have control over and how you're going to deliver them. For example, what physical evidence (reviews) you can use to promote your new book, and where you're going to promote it (online, traditional media, in person), which people you need to work with to ensure your marketing mix is integrated – your publisher, a local library etc.
- Work through the process to identify your readers, described in Chapter 10. Understand her values, likes, dislikes, what excites her. Write a profile for your typical reader. Make sure all your communications with your readers work for this reader. Go to your readers, don't expect them to come to you!
- Use the knowledge about your typical reader to plan your next book marketing campaign as in Chapter 12. Where will you place articles, where will you hang out in person and online? Suggest these to your publisher.
- Think about marketing planning as described in Chapter 4 – analyse the wider environment – political, social, technological etc. Use this to inform the topic / theme / promotion etc of your next book.
- Think about your marketing communications, in Chapter 4. Now you know who your typical reader is,

ensure all your marketing communications DRIP. Every tweet, Facebook post, every book cover, online image to promote your book, blog, flyers anything that communicates with readers about your book.

- Use the knowledge of who your readers are, and the trends in entertainment to write your next book based on anticipating reader demand, Chapter 4, semi-programmed issue.

- If all this marketing speak is somewhat depressing and you feel like it's taking you away from the joy of writing, I apologise for that. It was never my intention. However, please remember that a romance book is a product just like a packet of cereal, a pair of shoes or a car; take some time to learn about the genre expectations so you ensure your books meet readers' expectations and lead them wanting to return for more, but different. It's perfectly possible to tell essentially the same story in a myriad of different ways, without becoming staid. Remember, only you can write *your* story in *your* voice in *your* way. If you gave twelve authors the basic plot of Cinderella and asked them to write a 50,000 word story based on it, you'd get twelve different stories, 24 different main character combinations (imagine a male male or a female female Cinderella story) and twelve different author voices. Which is what's so wonderful about being an author. But rest assured, if one of the stories ended with Cinderella dying or the prince disappearing into the sunset with one of the evil step sisters, despite Cinderella being made for the prince, that story would certainly not have most readers returning for more from that author.

- Analyse your own writing and see if you're giving your readers reasons to return as described in Chapter 10 – the emotional highs, the effortlessness of reading, an escapist quality while being grounded in a reality readers recognise. If you're finding it hard to find an agent or a publisher for your story it may be linked to these factors. Although beautifully written, there may not be enough emotion to interest a romance reader. You may be trying to be too clever with your prose rather than saying what you mean and getting on with delivering the story to the reader. Does your romance novel follow the structure of a commercial fiction story – gradually building tension with a peak before resolving and reducing the tension? If your story bumbles along at a middle or low level of tension, it won't meet the structure romance readers have come to expect, and hence won't be of interest to agents or publishers in this competitive, highly customer-led genre.

Well, that's all from me, I hope I've demystified marketing and explained how romance is a marketing-led and therefore customer-led genre.

Happy marketing and most importantly, happy writing!

Love and light, Liam Livings xx

Bibliography

Non-Fiction Books

Asimov, J. & A. (1987). *How To Enjoy Writing A book of Aid and Comfort.* New York: The Walker Publishing Company, Inc.

Booker, C. (2004). *The seven basic plots of literature.* New York: Continuum.

Christopher, Martin; Payne, Adrian and Ballantyne, David (1991) *Relationship Marketing,* Oxford: Butterworth-Heineman Ltd.

King, G. (2009). *Collins improve your writing skills.* Glasgow: Harper Collins Publishers.

Radway, J. (1991). *Reading the Romance: Women, Patriarchy, and Popular Literature.* University of North Carolina Press.

Regis, P. (2013). *A Natural History of the Romance Novel.* Philadelphia: University of Pennsylvania Press.

Vivanco, L. (2011). *For Love and Money.* Humanities-Ebooks.

Fiction Books

Bagwell, S. (2014). *One Tall, Dusty Cowboy.* London: Mills and Boon.

Bolter, A. (2017). *Her New York Billionaire.* London: Mills and Boon.

Coleridge, N. (2010). *Deadly Sins.* London: Orion.

Collins, J. (2012). *The Power Trip.* London: Simon & Shuster UK Ltd.

Cooper, J. (1977) *Octavia.* London: Corgi Books.

Cooper, J. (1993). *The Man Who Made Husbands Jealous.* Corgi.

Cooper, J. (2015) (originally 1985) Riders. London: Transworld Publishers.

Evans, H. (2011). *Love Always.* London: HarperCollins Publishers.

Fox, V. (2013). *Wicked Ambition.* Richmond: Harlequin Mira.

Green, J. (2012). *The Patchwork Marriage.* London: Pan Books.

Green, J. (2014). *Saving Grace*. London: Pan Books.

Hampton, S. (2014). *Back in Her Husband's Arms*. Richmond: Mills and Boon.

Jordan, P. (1985). *The six-month marriage*. London: Mills and Boon Ltd.

Jordan, P. (1998) (originally 1993). *Yesterday's Echoes*. London: Mills and Boon Ltd.

Jordan, p. (2012). *A secret disgrace*. Richmond: Harlequin Mills & Boon.

Keyes, M. (1997). *Rachel's Holiday*. London: Penguin Books.

Keyes, M. (2001). Sushi for Beginners. London: Penguin.

Leigh, A. (2015). *Fortune's June Bride*. Richmond: Mills and Boon.

Ley, R. (2014). *Return to Mandalay*. London: Quercus Editions Ltd.

Merman, E. and Eells, G. (1978). *Merman – An Autobiography*. New York: Simon & Schuster.

Parks, A. (2012). *About Last Night*. Headline Review.

Pearson, A. (2011). *I don't know how she does it*. Vintage.

Pembroke, S. (2015). *Falling For The Bridesmaid*. Richmond: Mills and Boon.

Roberts, N. (2011) (originally 1990). *Dance to the Piper*. Richmond: Silhouette Books.

Sparks, M. (1961). *The Prime Of Miss Jean Brodie*. London, Penguin.

Susann, J (2003) (originally 1966). *Valley of the Dolls*. London: Virago Press.

Trollope, J. (1994). *A Spanish Lover*. Black Swan.

Trollope, J. (1999). *Other People's Children*. Black Swan.

Vincenzi, P. (2006). *Into Temptation*. Headline Review.

Vincenzi, P. (2009). *An Absolute Scandal*. New York: Anchor Books.

Other printed references
Conde Nast Traveller – The 20th Anniversary Issue, October 2017, London: Conde Nast.

Online references

BBC, (1993) *A Is For ABBA Documentary. Available at: https://www.youtube.com/watch?v=XUlw3A-A3Rg*

Berlatsky, N. (2014). *Why Don't Men Read Romance Novels?. [online] Pacific Standard. Available at: https://psmag.com/social-justice/dont-men-read-romance-novels-misogyny-femininity-publishing-books-92921 [Accessed 18 Sep. 2017].*

Bernazzani, S. (2016) *11 Examples of Facebook Ads That Actually Work (And Why). Available at: https://blog.hubspot.com/blog/tabid/6307/bid/33319/10-examples-of-facebook-ads-that-actually-work-and-why.aspx*

Blank, D. (2017). *3 Unconventional Ways to Use Social Media to Find Readers. [online] The Creative Penn. Available at: https://www.thecreativepenn.com/2017/03/16/social-media-to-find-readers*

CIM 2015, Marketing and the 7Ps: A brief summary of marketing and how it work, available at https://www.cim.co.uk/media/4772/7ps.pdf

Clark, K. (2012). *Features, Advantages, and Benefits | FAB Statements - devEdge Blog. [online] devEdge Internet Marketing. Available at: http://devedge-internet-marketing.com/2012/10/06/features-advantages-and-benefits-fab-statements/*

Dalke, R. (2016). *The Business Of Romance Novels. Available at: http://u.osu.edu/dalke6hseportfolio/files/2016/04/The-Business-of-Romance-Novels-Presentation-1t534ld.pdf*

Faircloth, K. (2017). *Here's How Not To Critique Romance Novels, Jezebel, available at https://jezebel.com/heres-how-not-to-critique-romance-novels-1819188174*

Flood, A. (2010). *An insider's guide to writing for Mills & Boon. [online] the Guardian. Available at: https://www.theguardian.com/books/2010/feb/15/insider-guide-writing-mills-boon*

Guy, D. (2016). *2016 Romance Writers of America RWA PAN Presentation. Available at: http://authorearnings.com/2016-rwa-pan-presentation/*

Hanlon, A. (2017). *How to use Segmentation, Targeting and Positioning (STP) to develop marketing strategies. Smart Insights.* Available at: http://www.smartinsights.com/digital-marketing-strategy/customer-segmentation-targeting/segmentation-targeting-and-positioning/

Harper, J. (2017). *Putting the 'commercial' into commercial fiction. Take Five Authors.* Available at: https://takefiveauthors.wordpress.com/2017/04/14/putting-the-commercial-into-commercial-fiction/

Jacoby, D. (n.d.). *Avoid Feature Dumping, Here's How Satisfy Your Customer.* [online] Salesreadinessgroup.com. Available at: https://www.salesreadinessgroup.com/avoiding-feature-dumping-how-to-satisfy-your-customer

Marsh, B. (2013). *A Brand is a Promise: 3 great examples of strong brands that make strong promises. Bill Marsh Junior Making You Matter,* available at http://www.billmarshjr.com/a-brand-is-a-promise-3-great-examples-of-strong-brands-that-make-strong-promises/

Mayo, K. (2014). *Dear columnists, romance fiction is not your bitch. ABC News.* Available at http://www.abc.net.au/news/2014-04-17/mayo-dear-columnists,-romance-fiction-is-not-your-bitch/5396672

Mills and Boon, (n.d.) *Paperback subscriptions models,* Available at: https://www.millsandboon.co.uk/np/subscriptions/paperback-subscription

Oliver, S. (2015). *Mills & Boon: And you thought romance was dead!.* Available at: http://www.dailymail.co.uk/home/event/article-3147237/Mills-Boon-thought-romance-dead-35-000-tender-clinches-30-000-kisses-10-000-s-Mills-Boon-booming-100-years-on.html

Patterson, A. (2016). *The 17 Most Popular Genres In Fiction - And Why They Matter - Writers Write.* [online] Available at: https://writerswrite.co.za/the-17-most-popular-genres-in-fiction-and-why-they-matter/

Quora, (n.d.) *Who Wrote The Quote, "If I had more time, I would have written you a shorter letter."?* Available at: https://www.quora.com/Who-wrote-the-quote-If-I-had-more-time-I-would-have-written-you-a-shorter-letter

Jeffers, R. (2008). About The Romance Genre from Romance Writers of America, available at http://www.rjeffers.com/romancegenre.pdf

Rodale, M. (2015). Who Is The Romance Novel Reader, Huffington Post, Available at http://www.huffingtonpost.com/maya-rodale/who-is-the-the-romance-novel-reader_b_7192588.html

The RNA, (n.d.). http://www.romanticnovelistsassociation.org/

The RWA, (2014). The Romance Book Buyer, Available at: https://www.rwa.org/p/cm/ld/fid=582

Vahl, A. (2014). The Truth About Facebook Ads: Do They Actually Work? 60 Second Marketer. Available at: http://60secondmarketer.com/blog/2013/11/04/do-facebook-ads-work/

VW, (1987), VW Golf Paula Hamilton Advert, available here https://www.youtube.com/watch?v=gKQIUJOr1GA

Wijitha.blogspot.co.uk. (2009). Top 100 Global Brands of 2008 and their Slogans. [online] Available at: http://wijitha.blogspot.co.uk/2009/01/top-100-global-brands-of-2008-and-their.html

Yardley, C. (2015). Fiction Writers: How to Find Your Ideal Reader - The Book Designer. [online] The Book Designer. Available at: https://www.thebookdesigner.com/2015/02/fiction-writers-how-to-find-your-ideal-reader

Printed in Poland
by Amazon Fulfillment
Poland Sp. z o.o., Wrocław